in small things
forgotten

an archaeology of early american life

EXPANDED AND REVISED

anchor books

doubleday

NEW YORK LONDON TORONTO SYDNEY AUCKLAND

james deetz

illustrated by amy elizabeth grey

in small things

forgotten

AN ANCHOR BOOK
PUBLISHED BY DOUBLEDAY
a division of Bantam Doubleday Dell Publishing
Group, Inc.
1540 Broadway, New York, New York 10036

ANCHOR BOOKS, DOUBLEDAY, and the portrayal of
an anchor are trademarks of Doubleday, a division
of Bantam Doubleday Dell Publishing Group, Inc.

Book design by Jennifer Ann Daddio

Library of Congress Cataloging-in-Publication Data

Deetz, James.
In small things forgotten : an archaeology of early
American life / James Deetz ; illustrated by Amy
Elizabeth Grey. — Rev. and expanded ed.
p.   cm.
1. New England—Antiquities.   2. New England—
Social life and customs—To 1775.   3. Virginia—
Antiquities.   4. Virginia—Social life and customs—
To 1775.   5. Archaeology and history—New
England.   6. Archaeology and history—Virginia.
I. Title.
F6.D43   1996
974′.01—dc20   96-1739
                                                      CIP

ISBN 0-385-48399-6
FIRST ANCHOR BOOKS EDITION: 1977
EXPANDED AND REVISED ANCHOR BOOKS EDITION:
1996
9   10   8

contents

To my dear friends and valued colleagues

Henry Glassie and Trish Scott

and

Henry Burlingame, Ebenezer Cooke, and

Joan Toast, my fellow Marylanders

introduction

There are times in all of our lives when things take a different turn, when we look at them from a new perspective, and depart from the path which had been followed. For me, one such time was on Halloween night, 1969, in Toledo, Ohio. I was attending an American Studies conference, where a panel discussion had been convened to consider what contribution, if any, historical archaeology might make to that field of scholarship. I was a member of the panel, as was Wilcomb Washburn; I no longer remember who the others were. Late that afternoon, I was approached by a student who asked if I had met Henry Glassie. I replied that I had not, although I had read his recently published *Pattern in the Material Folk Culture of the Eastern United States* and discovered for the first time the world of folk life studies and how they related to the research I had been doing. My work included studies of mortuary art in old New England cemeteries, and the excavation of a number of colonial sites in the Plymouth Colony area; but it lacked a center. It was unfocused in many ways. I had recently introduced a new course at Brown University, American Material Culture, and in the first few years that I taught it, it was similarly uncentered, being a kind of free-ranging discussion of everything from old houses to ceramics.

Henry and I were introduced in the lobby of the hotel where the conference was being held, and as is usual on such occasions, we adjourned to the bar. I learned that he had been using my *Invitation to Archaeology* in one of his courses, and had found it to be relevant in many ways to his research interests. So it was that a kind of intellectual fusion took place as the conversation developed, lasting through dinner. I think we both realized that we were doing much the same thing, even though we were from separate and seemingly different disciplines. From that date on, Henry and I continued what has become a twenty-seven-year collegial relationship. I have always thought of him as my intellectual mentor. I have made free use of his many ideas, and like to think that at least to some degree, the relationship has been reciprocal.

Over the next few years, the material culture course at Brown was transformed and greatly improved, due largely to my incorporating insights gained from Henry. By 1972, it had assumed the form which it was to retain through four more years at Brown, fourteen years at Berkeley, and most recently, the last three years at the University of Virginia. In 1975, I felt confident enough with the material to write it down in book form, and in 1977 it was published as *In Small Things Forgotten*. I have been very pleased by the reception that the book has been given, and like to think that it has provided its thousands of readers with some idea of what we do as historical archaeologists. But in the nineteen years that have passed since its first appearance, I have shifted my area of research from New England to the Chesapeake, and although I have incorporated this later work in my teaching, *In Small Things Forgotten* has remained largely a book on New England historical archaeology. This revised and expanded version has been produced to incorporate more recent material which has become a standard part of my course. I hope that it succeeds.

One of the more important developments in American historical archaeology during the past two decades has been the emergence of African American archaeology as a critical component of the field. The organization and content of the present book reflect this, but presenting the material does pose a problem. Is it better to discuss aspects of African American archaeology integrated with that which treats the European American experience, or should it be set apart? Both have merit, but I have chosen the latter, since I believe that in so doing, one attains a better appreciation of the way in which various facets of a cultural whole are related and integrated than if they were related piecemeal to those of another, different cultural configuration, particularly if the latter is that of the dominant group. A secondary problem is one of terminology. The reader will notice that two terms, African and African American, are used in the text in what might seem a rather random fashion. This is actually not the case. In many instances, particularly when one is discussing the seventeenth century, the probability that a significant portion of people of African descent actually were born in Africa is quite high. In other cases, one cannot be so sure. I have tried to use "African" in those places where I believe the people in question to have been of African origin, and "African American" where there is a considerable degree of ambiguity.

In the course of revising and expanding *In Small Things Forgotten,* I have benefited from conversations with a number of people. Some read portions of the manuscript, especially Chapter Eight, and others made helpful and constructive suggestions on subjects ranging from African house framing techniques to the potential economic implications of inexpensive mass-produced Staffordshire ceramics. For this, I thank Anna Agbe-Davies, Alison Bell, Eric Deetz, Garret Fesler, Maria Franklin, Jeff Hantman, Bill Kelso, Nick Luccketti, Seth Mallios, Fraser Neiman, Trish Scott, Mark Warner, and Derek Wheeler. Trish Scott did a monumental job of transferring my poorly typed manuscript to disk, and setting it in a clear and concise format. Without her assistance, this book would have been at least another year in coming. At Doubleday, Papatya Bucak has been everything one could ask of an editor. Amy Grey took on illustrating the book on somewhat short notice, and did an elegant job of transforming murky photographs and sometimes less than crisp photocopies into figures which are as professional as they are lovely. Finally, I am sincerely grateful to my colleagues at the University of Virginia and the people of Charlottesville for providing an environment which made the writing of this revision a genuinely enjoyable experience.

Charlottesville
December 1995

in small things
forgotten

recalling things forgotten:
archaeology and
the american artifact

CHARLOTTESVILLE, VIRGINIA, 1780

Little Isaac Jefferson watched as his mother prepared their evening meal in the tiny slave cabin which was home. As pastry chef in the big house at Monticello, she was familiar with European ways of cooking, but here at home she was doing something quite different. Two pots simmered by the fire. Handmade and unglazed, they were gray-brown in color. The larger held a thick porridge of dried corn, the smaller a rich mixture of herbs, tomatoes, and bits of rabbit and squirrel. Their contents would be served together in shallow bowls.

PORTSMOUTH, RHODE ISLAND, 1745

The job had been a big one, and the house carpenter had been at it for over a month. Now complete, Jacob Mott's farmhouse had a new wing and a new look. The old, projecting end of the second floor of the house had been removed, and the location of the door had been changed. Standing back to view his work, the carpenter noticed how much more the house now seemed like those in the center of town. Although it stood in the middle of more than a hundred acres of farmland tilled by the Mott family, its new face would tell the people of Portsmouth that Jacob Mott was one of them, just as though he lived as their next-door neighbor.

PLYMPTON, MASSACHUSETTS, 1765

Ebenezer Soule set down his hammer and chisel. It was late evening, but he had completed the gravestone that he had been carving and that now stood before him. On its top he had carved a cheerful angel's face, and he thought of how it would look when it was placed over the grave the next day. Although he had been making gravestones for years, this design was new to him. He knew that the people in the area had recently come to prefer cherubs on their monuments, and lately he had been carving more and more of them to meet the new demand.

INDEPENDENCE, VIRGINIA, 1932

Since his return from a trip to Tennessee, Wade Ward had been practicing a new way to play his banjo. Placing his fingers across all four strings high on the neck, he picked out a series of notes, then repeated the sequence farther down the fretboard. The day before, making music with his nephew Fields, he had alternated the style he had used since childhood—striking the strings with the nails of his right hand—with another new trick: picking up with his fingertips. In doing this he was playing his banjo as the musicians did on so many of the new records that people listened to on their radios almost every day.

KINGSTON, MASSACHUSETTS, 1765
The ads in the Boston newspapers had announced a new shipment of English china. William Rand made a special trip from his home in Kingston to Boston, where he purchased a dozen matching blue-and-white plates. They would make a handsome addition to his household and complement the new set of matching chairs he had recently acquired for his dining room.

FLOWERDEW HUNDRED, VIRGINIA, 1695
From the outside, the house gave the appearance of substance and permanence, down to the fine casements of leaded windowpanes. But its owner, John Limbrey Wilkins, knew better. The house was framed on stout posts which were set deep into the ground without benefit of footings. In having the house built in this fashion, Wilkins was able to save a substantial amount of capital, which he felt was better directed to producing a tobacco crop which would give him a handsome return on his investment. After all . . .

PLYMOUTH, MASSACHUSETTS, 1658
The appraiser appointed by the court worked slowly and carefully from room to room in the small, dimly lit house.

Its owner had recently died, and his property had to be valued so that a proper tax could be levied on his estate. The list covered several pages: chairs, fireplace equipment, beds, napkins, chests, clothing—all of the property that had been used to make the world a more comfortable place in which to live. At the end of the listing, the appraiser made a final entry: "In small things forgotten, eight shillings six-pence." In this he acknowledged things that he may have overlooked but that nevertheless had value.

Seven Americans engaged in commonplace activities; all in their fashion were communicating with us in a subtle way. In each case, material objects were involved—a house, a gravestone, a set of dishes—and if we could in some way find a way to understand the significance of artifacts as they were thought of and used by Americans in the past, we might gain new insight into the history of our nation.

Such a concern for the material objects of the past, the "small things forgotten," is central to the work of historical archaeologists. Archaeology is the study of past peoples based on the things they left behind and the ways they left their imprint on the world. Chipped-stone hand axes made hundreds of thousands of years ago and porcelain teacups from the eighteenth century carry messages from their makers and users. It is the archaeologist's task to decode those messages and apply them to our understanding of the human experience. Modern American culture, a rich and vibrant blend of African, Asian, European, and Native

American cultural traditions, is studied by folklorists, historians, sociologists, and anthropologists. Historical archaeology can add to our understanding of the American experience in a unique way, by looking not at the written record alone but at the almost countless objects left behind by Americans for over three and a half centuries.

Historical archaeology studies the cultural remains of literate societies that were capable of recording their own histories. In this respect it contrasts directly with prehistoric archaeology, which treats all of cultural history before the advent of writing, millions of years in duration. A popular definition of historical archaeology is *the archaeology of the spread of European cultures throughout the world since the fifteenth century, and their impact on and interaction with the cultures of indigenous peoples.* Two things should be noted regarding this definition. First, the words "throughout the world" take on special significance when comparisons are made with prehistoric archaeology. By and large, prehistorians do not think on a scale that is truly global, and have no need to operate on such a scale. However, historical archaeology must adopt a global perspective on its data, for when the first European sailing ships set out for distant parts of the world, a chain of events never before seen in human history was set into motion. Two worlds that had been separate from each other for millennia suddenly were brought into close contact, with spectacular and often catastrophic results. This contact leads to the second point. The millions of Africans who were transported to the Americas were relocated, against their will, as a direct result of European colonial expansion into the New World. In like manner, the Asian presence in America came as a result of American expansion westward, and while the particular circumstances were different, the end result was the same. As such, both African American and Asian American archaeology are integral components of American historical archaeology, as is the history of the Native American peoples following the initial contact with European peoples.

In England, studies of sites and artifacts that relate to Anglo-American sites are done by *postmedieval archaeologists*. Their work and that of historical archaeologists in America tell the story of the development of Anglo-American culture from its English beginnings to its ultimate twentieth-century form in North America. The examples to be examined in this volume will treat the Americanization of both English and African traditions as this was played out along the eastern seaboard during colonial and postcolonial times. To be sure, other European nations were involved in the colonization of North America—notably Spain, France, and Holland—and the bearers of their cultural traditions interacted with those of others as well, but this volume will restrict its concerns to only two, to illustrate the workings of historical archaeology as it is actually practiced in the United States.

It is in its sharp contrasts with prehistoric archaeology that historical archaeology may be further defined. Not only do the two disciplines treat complementary sets of data, based on the presence or absence of literacy and written records, but they differ in other critical ways which are only partly a result of this essential difference.

Testimony of the Spade, Still Digging, Archaeology from the Earth—all are titles of books by prehistorians which reflect the near identity in most people's minds between archaeology and excavation. This is so simply because the vast majority of human cultural remains *are* buried and must be dug up. But the excavation of archaeological sites, though an obviously essential first step in studying past cultures, is just that. Only after the material has been excavated can we begin to study it.

Because historical archaeologists work with materials that are centuries old at most, rather than millennia or longer periods, these materials stand a much better chance of surviving above the ground. Of course, much of historical archaeology *is* the digging of archaeological sites, but these sites are not the sole source of information. They can provide information that is not available from other sources, and the value of this material is further enhanced through the support of aboveground information. For example, there is no need to detail the architecture of early New England timber-framed houses on the basis of excavated material alone, since the landscape is dotted with such buildings, still standing and in use.

Like old houses, there are certain other artifacts from America's past available for study, but their value is subject to certain limitations, which must be kept in mind. Collections in museums have preserved a vast wealth of American artifacts: ceramics, metalwork, and glassware have their archaeological counterparts, and many materials that the archaeologist rarely has access to, such as leather, paper, fabric, and wood, are also available for study. The question of the factors that favor survival of certain objects and the disappearance of others is important here. For a variety of reasons, surviving artifacts cannot be taken as necessarily representative objects of their period. If we were to rely on museum collections, we might get an impression of a much richer level of material wealth than truly was the case. This is because most museums save the unusual and the valuable object, and individuals now and in the past consign commonplace objects to the dump. A museum exhibit of all of the pottery found in a household of modest means in the mid eighteenth century would not be beautiful to behold, since most of it would be simple, locally manufactured, coarse earthenware, red in color and undecorated. But such an exhibit would certainly be representative of the world of the people who lived in it. In a similar way, we often are told that old garments, shoes, or pieces of armor show definitely that "people were smaller in those days." This conclusion does not allow for the probability that very small items of personal wear would not be as eligible for hand-me-down status, and thus were less likely to wear out. The houses that survive from the seventeenth and eighteenth centuries also cannot be taken at face value as typical of their time, since their ruder counterparts almost certainly disappeared from the scene in a short time. Indeed, Jack Larkin tells us that according to the 1798 Direct Tax, which described every free families' dwelling house, the American housing landscape was "striking in its small scale, its plainness and its inequality."[1] Most families lived in houses of one or possibly two rooms, and these have mostly disappeared.

As historical archaeologists work in increasingly more recent periods, they find on occasion an information source that few if any prehistorians have encountered: the archaeological informant. Since the period with which historical archaeology is concerned extends to the present, the last seventy-odd years can be studied through direct interviews with people who actually experienced the lifeways being studied. Memory, of course, is fallible, and whenever possible, it is best to conduct interviews with more than one person for corroborative purposes.

The widespread use of photography by the mid nineteenth century provides the historical archaeologist with another valuable data source. Buildings that have long since vanished and landscapes that have been transformed can be seen in old photographs as they appeared at the time that the archaeologist is investigating if the site in question dates to the period when the photograph was taken. An ingenious use of photographs as an archaeological resource has been developed by Eugene Prince of the Phoebe Hearst Museum of the University of California at Berkeley.[2] The technique is simple in execution but dramatic in results. A historical photograph of a building or even an entire community is first made into a thirty-five-millimeter transparency. The transparency is then inserted in the prism mounting of a single-lens reflex, which enables one to see the photograph when looking through the viewfinder of the camera. One need only identify at least two reference points in the photograph on the modern landscape. Using these points and a zoom lens, since the focal length of the camera which took the original photograph is unknown, the camera is moved around until the reference points match. Once this has been done, the precise location of buildings, roads, or fence lines can be seen on the modern landscape. It is even possible to have people "enter" the historical photograph and measure a building or buildings that are no longer in existence. The technique has been used successfully to identify the precise point where Ulysses S. Grant's army crossed the James River en route to Petersburg, to check the accur.cy of a restoration at Colonial Williamsburg, and to locate an early-nineteenth-century shipyard at Fort Ross, California, photographed in 1862. Archaeological investigations at the abandoned coal mining town of Somersville, California, were immensely aided through the use of this technique. With a panoramic view of the town, it was possible to pinpoint all of the buildings and fence lines. With additional information obtained from oral history accounts, it was possible to construct a very accurate map of the town, when none had existed before.

The literacy of the people it studies is what sets historical archaeology apart from prehistory. But not all the people were able to read and write; indeed only a minority could through most of the time with which we are concerned. But even if a majority lacked the ability to write, others often wrote about them. They were born, married, and died, and these events were recorded; their estates were listed for tax purposes and so were recorded. The church records, diaries, court records, land deeds, and contemporary histories give us a window through which to witness the past. This is not to say that we can learn all there is to know just from studying the written record. If this were so, there would be no need to dig into the ground or to sort, measure, and classify artifacts. In spite of the richness and diversity of the historical record, there are things we want to know that are not to be discovered from it. Simple people doing simple things, the normal, everyday routine of life and how these people thought about it, are not the kinds of things anyone thought worthy of noting. We know far more about the philosophical underpinnings of Puritanism than we do about what its practitioners consumed at countless meals. But all left behind the material residue of their existence, and it, too, is worth study. As Henry Glassie says of the folks of middle Virginia: "They left no writing, but they did leave all those houses."[3]

The documentary record and the archaeological record complement each other. One of the most useful sets of written material is probate records. These are listings, of the contents of the houses and properties of persons, taken for tax purposes at their deaths. Although not every estate was probated—more often only the richer estates were—those inventories that we have access to are valuable for a number of reasons. Hundreds of thousands of inventories exist for the Anglo-American world. They usually take the form of a rather detailed listing of the contents of a person's estate, with accompanying values. The inventory of Thomas Lumbert's estate, which follows, is an example.

The Inventory of Thomas Lumbert

A true Inventory of the estate of Thomas Lumbert of Barnstable senir: deceased; exhibited to the Court held att Plymouth March the seauenth 1664 on the oath of Ioyce Lumbert widdow;

	li	s	d
Impr in Lands and housing	60	00	00
Item 2 oxen	12	00	00
Item 5 Cowes	19	10	00
Item 1 heiffer	03	00	00
Item 4 yearlings	04	10	00
Item 2 Calues	00	10	00
Item 2 oxen 12 li and six pound in [vse?] laied out for meddow	18	00	00
Item 2 mares	15	00	00
Item 1 mare Colt	03	00	00
Item 2 horses	14	00	00
Item a two yeare old Colt	04	[10]	00
Item 1 yearling Calfe	02	10	00
Item swine	01	00	00

in small things forgotten

Item his wearing clothes	03	10	00
Item in beding and yearne	07	15	00
Item in linnine	02	00	00
Item in brasse potts and kettles	03	10	00
Item one warming pan	00	08	00
Item 1 frying pan 3s 1 Iron kettle 3s and hangers 1s6d	00	07	06
Item Cubbert and Chistes	01	00	00
Item Chernes barrells tubbs treyes and such like lumber	01	05	00
Item bookes	00	14	00
Item Amunition	04	00	00
Item in a saddle and bridle	00	12	00
Item in flesh meale and prouision for the family	01	15	00
Item in Corne and pease	01	12	00
Item in Cart wheeles plough and plow tackling	04	00	00

Item in Carpenters tooles	03	00	00
Item the loomes	00	10	00
Item in sythes hoes wedges old Iron- mattock & such like thinges	01	00	00
Item in debtes due	[16]	00	00
February the 8th 1664)	210	08	06
more in triuiall thinges omited	00	10	00
To debts owing to seuerall men	10	00	00

henerey Cobb
Iohn Gorum
Nathaniel Bacon

Ioyce Lumbert was deposed to the truth of this Inventory; soe farr as shee knowes) before mee Thomas hinckley this sixt of March (64)

65

The uses of inventories transcend the obvious, descriptive one. The terms used in the inventories are those used by the people themselves, and as such constitute what is known as a folk taxonomy. This can be very misleading on occasion. Numerous listings of "looking glasses" in inventories of early-seventeenth-century Plymouth might

in small things forgotten

lead the reader to believe there was a good supply of mirrors. While this is possible, we learn from the Oxford English Dictionary that "looking glass" was a common vernacular term for chamber pot during the first half of the seventeenth century. "Bedstead" at this time denotes what we call a bed, and "bed" in the folk taxonomy refers to what we would call a mattress. The adjective "coarse" did not denote texture until late in the seventeenth century; earlier, it meant normal or average. It is therefore necessary that one become familiar with the semantics of the English language during the period under study.

A significant number of inventories were taken on a room-by-room basis, and as such give us not only an idea of the layout of the house but the terms used for its various rooms. In such cases, the objects listed for various rooms also hint at the activities that went on in them.

But the inventories always stop short of the kind of detail that the archaeologist often finds important. A listing of earthenware could refer either to fancy, imported pottery or to plain coarse ware of local manufacture. "Six old spoons" might have been of either pewter or brass, and even if the material is mentioned, there was a variety of styles of spoons in use at any one time. In many ways the inventories are given detail by what is excavated from the earth. Taken together, inventories and archaeological assemblages give a more detailed and complete picture than either could alone.

So it is with many other types of recorded information. Building contracts often give specific descriptions of the house or barn to be constructed. The following is a good example:

> Thomas Joy hath an account against Mr Robert Keayne for Doing the Carpentry worke of a Barne at Mr Keaynes house at Rumney Marsh & for setting up & finishing the same being of 72 foot in length & 26 foot wide & 10 foot high wth 2 porches each of 13 foot wide one way & 12 another for wch the said Tho: J alleageth he ought to be payd so much as the Carpentry worke thereof is worth and he saith that the said worke comes unto in value as followeth in particulares vizt the framing of the said barne 30£ the sawing thereof 17£. The felling crosse cutting & squaring of the timber 15£ and more the rearing up of the barne by him & his servants 7 the clapboarding of the barne 11£ 5s for boards 4£ 16s for laying of 600 of boards over the porches 18s for making of 4 payre of great doores & hanging of them 2£ for making of two paire of stayres 6s for making of four little doors 6s for laying the barne floare wth plancks 600£ 10s for putting on gutters upon the barne 1£ 10s for ferrayge of him and his servants 2 10s for losse of time in going and comming 4£ wch comes in all to 98£ 1s
>
> (A 1640 CONTRACT, BETWEEN THOMAS JOY AND ROBERT KEAYNE, FOR A BARN TO BE ERECTED IN RUMNEY MARSH, ESSEX COUNTY, MASSACHUSETTS)

Even the court records provide us with information concerning architecture. Certain important details are supplied by two ~~coroners' inquests~~ in seventeenth-century Plymouth:

> Wee declare, y^t coming into the house of the said Richard Bishope, wee saw at the foot of a ~~ladder wch leadeth into an vpper chamber,~~ much blood; and going vp all of vs into the chamber, wee found a woman child, of about foure years . . .
>
> (AN INQUEST HELD AT PLYMOUTH, MASSACHUSETTS, 1648; *PLYMOUTH COLONY RECORDS, II, COURT ORDERS*, P. 133)

> . . . they sent vp into the chamber by one of the children, whoe cried out that his mother is hanging herselfe; whereupon the said Elizabeth and Robert ran vp . . . and there found an haire rope or halter, fastened very feirme to ~~the collar beame~~ . . .
>
> (VERDICT OF CORONER'S JURY RE SUICIDE OF THE WIFE OF JAMES CLAGHORNE, YARMOUTH, MASSACHUSETTS, 1677; *PLYMOUTH COLONY RECORDS, V, COURT ORDERS*, P. 249)

In the first example, we learn of the use of a ladder rather than stairs to gain access to an upper chamber. The second tells us that collar beams were used, typical of one of several roof-framing techniques.

As we can see from the three examples above, historical archaeology must work with parallel and related sets of information. Yet in some cases there is a disturbing contradiction between what is excavated and what is written down. For example, listings of livestock often do not reflect the ratios of various species that are turned up by excavating animal bones in sites of the same period. This is because not all livestock was used as a meat source. Early Plymouth supported its economy in large measure by trading cattle to Massachusetts Bay Colony; the islands in Narragansett Bay were used to raise vast herds of sheep for export to the West Indies. In neither case would the actual frequency of one species to another appear in excavated animal bone, since the latter reflects only those animals consumed as food.

A second kind of accommodation between excavated materials and documentary information bears directly on the whole complex problem of artifact typology as it is practiced by prehistorians. The classification of the artifacts recovered from a prehistoric site is a critical initial step in any archaeological analysis. In briefest terms, typology involves the classification of objects based on similarity of form; triangular arrowheads are different from those with curved sides; pots painted red on white are different from those painted black on red. Such classification allows controlled comparison between collections from different sites. But such classifications are entirely formal, and arrived at, by necessity, independently of what the makers of the objects perceived as different types. With the rich documentary materials of historical archaeology, such classifications are not only sterile exercises but potentially very misleading. European-made ceramics excavated from Anglo-American sites are complex and very diverse, but since so much research has been done on the history of the pottery industry in England and continental Europe, it is not unusual to know how the makers of this pottery classified, named, and traded their wares. ~~To apply strictly formal classificatory methods to this material and ignore the historical data is like trying to reinvent the incandescent lamp by candlelight while ignoring the light switch at one's elbow.~~

A poor fit between the two above kinds of information forces researchers to refine their interpretations, to the benefit of the final results. At the same time, the historical sources have the potential to provide the archaeologist with a much more richly detailed statement of a past lifestyle, and with deeper and more sophisticated understandings of the workings and development of the American past.

If you were to visit a "typical" historical archaeological site, it would look not terribly different from its prehistoric counterpart. To be sure, the artifacts being recovered would be very different, but the use of excavation grids, trenches, and test pits would be identical. Field archaeology is based on observation. Earth is removed from the objects recovered to make observation more efficient. The same earth covers a seventeenth-century colonial foundation and a nearby prehistoric Indian shell heap, and the techniques for its removal are essentially the same. But the historical features and structures that are covered by this earth are so different from those found in many prehistoric sites that they demand a different excavation scheme.

Most historic sites are quite visible even before any digging is done. Mounds indicate collapsed chimneys, large stones marking wall footings often protrude through the sod, and frequently there are standing structural remains associated with those buried. At the most visible extreme, whole buildings form the focus of archaeological excavation, and the excavation must proceed in a manner coordinated with the analysis of the structures themselves. In the case of many prehistoric sites there is so little evidence of the area of occupation prior to digging that rather sophisticated sampling techniques are often required to ensure the proper location and recovery of significant information. Given the higher visibility of historic sites, such techniques are often unnecessary, and if used under such circumstances, can also be highly inefficient.

There are, of course, notable exceptions. An entire building tradition in the seventeenth-century Chesapeake has vanished leaving hardly a trace; only two examples have survived the passage of time. Known as earthfast or post-in-ground construction, this tradition involved framing the house on posts buried directly in the earth (see Figure 1). What has survived of houses of this type is little more than a faint pattern of soil stains, marking the location of the posts, to be seen only when the plowed earth has been removed, and then with difficulty. This building tradition was linked to a number of economic factors, to be

Figure 1. Earthfast or post-in-ground construction

discussed later, and was the commonest form of construction throughout the seventeenth century and in some places
into the eighteenth. Combined with frequent short supply
of essential goods, resulting in a thin refuse deposit, at

recalling things forgotten   21 times the absence of cellars, and hearth bases which were removed by plowing, this manner of building led to sites that are very difficult to detect from the surface. As a result, the field techniques used in excavating these sites more closely resemble those employed on prehistoric sites.

Another important difference between historic and prehistoric sites is the manner in which large quantities of fill, a mixture of soil and refuse, were shifted about in the historic period. This tendency has increased dramatically since the seventeenth century, as we can see from today's landfill projects, which are built up from refuse on a wholesale basis. Since such deposits invariably contain artifacts, they can be extremely misleading. An excavation of a large portion of a city block in downtown Providence, Rhode Island, encountered fill, with a rich artifact content, that had been hauled in from Attleboro, Massachusetts, some fifteen miles distant. Excavations in the rear of the post office in Plymouth, Massachusetts, on the supposed 1620 site of the Pilgrim William Brewster's first house, revealed nine feet of fill with seventeenth- and eighteenth-century artifacts, which had been originally excavated in another part of town. A park in New York City is composed partly of fill from Bristol, England, which was hauled in ships as ballast during the Battle of Britain. This refuse probably includes artifacts from the medieval period or earlier; the fact of the park's construction is noted on a plaque, yet this instance does illustrate in dramatic fashion how potentially misleading such wholesale shifting of large quantities of earth can be. In earlier times, technology was simpler, and large-scale filling was not common. Yet it occurred enough to require an accommodation for it in the digging of historic sites. Fill is an artifact itself, and intelligent study of it can be most instructive. This is particularly true in excavations carried out in high-density urban areas, where the same soil may have been removed, shifted, and redeposited many times.

A less dramatic example of how such filling might be misleading is the common tendency for people to have deposited large quantities of clean fill in privies, wells, cellars, and trash pits. In excavating a prehistoric site, once such clean soil is encountered, the base of the deposit probably has been reached. However, on historic sites, it is not uncommon to encounter soil that seems undisturbed but is in fact a deposit of sterile fill that might be three feet thick or more. Usually the edges of the pit in which it has been placed can be followed or an occasional fleck of charcoal or brick gives the lie to its apparent virginity, but on occasion such fill can be very deceptive.

Chronology in archaeology is one of the cornerstones for all analysis. The determination of the age of this or that archaeological site is critical before any consideration of process through time can be attempted. The battery of dating techniques available to the prehistorian is large and complex. Historical archaeology has different dating methods. Some methods, such as stratigraphy, which operates on the principle that archaeological deposits are laid down like layers of a cake, with the older ones deeper in the ground, are equally applicable in historical and prehistoric archaeology. Yet radiocarbon dating, a mainstay in prehistory, is of very limited use in historical archaeology, simply because the limits within which such dates are given are too general to be of much use to the historical archaeologist. A radiocarbon date in the seventeenth century might be stated as 1680 plus or minus forty or more years.

The more specialized dating techniques of historical archaeology can produce a much more precise statement of age. For example, the dates of manufacture of many English pottery types are known to within five years or less. If a cellar were excavated that contained fragments of creamware (an ivory-colored earthenware perfected by Josiah Wedgwood circa 1762), then the deposit in the cellar must be only as early as that date. The principle of dating such deposits on the basis of the newest artifact found in them is common to all of archaeology, both historic and prehistoric. Known as the *terminus post quem* (the date after which), this kind of dating is powerful when combined with a detailed knowledge of the history of the invention and development of the artifacts in question. The principle of the *terminus ante quem* (the date before which) is somewhat more difficult to apply, since any number of factors might account for the *absence* of a given artifact type. Nonetheless, it can be employed in historical archaeology with some confidence. A site that lacks creamware probably predates the 1770s, since by that time this pottery had become extremely common in England and America.

Extending the application of these principles to the great variety of artifacts of the historic period that is commonly encountered in the course of excavation provides the historical archaeologist with a very high degree of chronological control. Such dating precision in turn enables the construction of much more finely detailed chronologies and permits a correspondingly more specific description of culture change than one usually encounters in prehistory. Of course, with only three and a half centuries to work with, the need for chronological precision is greater than that for prehistory, which deals in greater time segments over a total period of millions of years.

The luxury of such detailed knowledge of the chronology of the pottery industry in Europe forms the basis of the Mean Ceramic Date Formula, a dating technique developed by Stanley South of the South Carolina Archaeology and Anthropology Institute.[4] The formula relies on the fact that the periods of manufacture of over a hundred pottery types are known. The first step in using the formula consists of counting all the fragments of each type from a site. Then we determine the mean manufacturing date for each type—the midpoint in the period when it was known to have been made. For example, if a kind of pottery was made between 1680 and 1740, the mean manufacturing date would be 1710, halfway between the two dates. These mean dates are assigned importance according to the relative quantity of each type of pottery at the site. An average of mean dates is taken, and the date that results should approximate the midpoint in the period when the site was occupied. The value of this technique is demonstrated in its use: it works. South applied it to a number of pottery collections from sites with known dates of occupation, with a resultant close match.

However, certain factors might introduce error in special cases. For example, if because of their social status, certain people either kept older pottery for a longer period of time or received hand-me-downs from their more affluent neighbors, the result would be an earlier date obtained from the formula than was actually so. The example is not purely theoretical. Excavations at the Parting Ways site, which was occupied by four families of freed slaves in Plymouth, Massachusetts, from circa 1785 through 1900, revealed a cellar that is thought to have been filled in upon its abandonment in 1850. The *terminus post quem* for the materials in the cellar is firmly established by a New England stoneware jar that bears the name of the maker, documented to have been working in Taunton, Massachusetts, in the 1840s. Yet the mean ceramic date of the cellar fill is 1794 by the South formula, while the actual mean occupation date would be circa 1822. In this case, independent archaeological and documentary information shows clearly that the occupants of the Parting Ways site were very poor, and for that reason could only have come by the rather fancy ceramics they owned through some second-hand way. However, what might at first appear as an erroneous date from the Mean Ceramic Date Formula could also be viewed as a potentially useful technique for the interpretation of archaeological remains. We have seen that when there is not a comfortable fit between archaeological and documentary materials, further questions are called

in small things forgotten

for. It follows that if the Mean Ceramic Date Formula were applied to sites for which the dates are independently determined, any major disagreement between these dates would require an explanation. The search for the explanation might well result in a better understanding of the material in cultural or behavioral terms.

The introduction of tobacco to England in the late sixteenth century led to a rapid development of the smoking-pipe industry. Pipes of white clay became extremely common, and sites in both England and America produce fragments of them by the thousands. Jean Harrington, an archaeologist working at Jamestown, noticed a definite relationship between the diameter of the bore of the pipestem and the age of the pipe of which it was a part. Pipes had earlier been dated on the basis of shapes of their bowls, but such a method was useless if only stem fragments were available; they are always far more numerous than bowls or whole pipes.

Using dated bowls with portions of their stems attached, Harrington discovered that the older the pipe, the larger the bore diameter of the stem. The earliest pipes, dating to about 1600, had stems with bores of $\frac{9}{64}$-inch diameter. By 1800 this diameter had decreased to $\frac{4}{64}$-inch. This change in diameter probably is due to the fact that pipestems became longer during this period, requiring a narrower bore diameter. This transformation in turn might ultimately relate to the greater availability of tobacco, which led to larger pipe bowls and potentially longer and hotter smokes. Lengthening the stem would remove the hot bowl farther from the mouth, and reducing the bore would cut down on the amount of matter transmitted through the stem to the smoker's mouth. Indeed, the early-seventeenth-century term for smoking was "drinking," and the method of smoking seems to have been much more hurried gulping of smoke from the small bowls typical of the period, with the relatively open stem bore allowing maximum transferral of the smoke to the mouth. The long, contemplative smoking of pipes with which we are so familiar today is probably of more recent origin.

Since the diameter of the stem bore slowly became smaller, apparently at a relatively uniform rate, this change provides the basis of a rather precise dating technique available to archaeologists working on Anglo-American sites of the seventeenth and eighteenth centuries. Using this method, the archaeologist has only to measure the diameter of the bores of pipestems from his site and compare the average bore diameters against a table that gives the average bore diameters for a number of periods. The time periods and average bore diameters are as follows:

Diameter	Dates
9/64	1590–1620
8/64	1620–1650
7/64	1650–1680
6/64	1680–1720
5/64	1720–1750
4/64	1750–1800

Suppose we have dug a site in which 70 percent of the stems have a bore diameter of 7/64 inch, 15 percent are 6/64 inch, and 15 percent 8/64 inch. This distribution would suggest that the site was occupied from 1650 to 1680. The few stems in the larger and smaller categories reflect either normal variation in bore diameter or a slightly longer time of occupation on either end of the period indicated by the majority of the stems. A refinement of this method using a simple and mathematical formula and yielding a single date, which can be thought of as being the middle of the occupation period, has been devised by Lewis Binford.[5]

Such a date is similar to that obtained from the Mean Ceramic Date Formula, and one can usually obtain both from a given collection. In most cases they will be approximately the same, lending mutual support. At present, the pipestem dating method is applicable only to pipes manufactured in England. Dutch pipes sometimes occur also on Anglo-American sites of the colonial period, but as yet a comparable chronology has not been established for the Dutch examples. In situations where the possibility of fragments of both Dutch and English pipestems exists, some error could be introduced into the data from this source.

We can see from the foregoing discussion that the basis for chronology in historical archaeology derives in one way or another from the greater independent control that can be marshaled from historical sources. The same applies to the wealth of primary documentary material, such as deeds, maps, diaries, and first-person histories, which often provides direct chronological information. If a house can be shown from recorded history to have been burned in 1676 during Bacon's Rebellion, and located accurately by researching land titles, then the archaeologist has as secure a *terminus ante quem* as he could ever hope for.

The wall trenches of a building beneath a standing wall of an extension to the Quaker meetinghouse in Newport, Rhode Island, must predate 1730, since church records tell us that the addition was built in that year. Given reliable documentation of this type, the urgency of deriving an artifactual *terminus post quem* or a mean ceramic date is lessened dramatically, although such independent information has strong corroborative value.

The historical archaeologist's approach to artifacts differs from the prehistorian's. Historical artifacts are vastly more diverse in terms of the materials from which they are made and their places of origin, which in North America commonly include such distant sources as China, the West Indies, and most of Europe. Much is known of their history and technology.[6]

On the one hand, then, the historical archaeologist enjoys the advantage of a detailed body of information concerning the artifacts, but, at the same time, it is essential that this information be controlled, which is no mean task. Yet it does remove the researcher from much of the formal analysis in which the prehistorian must become deeply involved. Given control of the necessary historical information, one can ultimately move on more easily and with a greater sense of security to the explanation of the artifacts

in small things forgotten

in terms of the society that used them. After all, this is the end toward which all archaeology is ultimately directed.

Finally, historical archaeology places less reliance on the natural sciences than does prehistoric archaeology. Not that the study of plant and animal remains, of soils, or of past climates has no place in historical archaeology; it emphatically does. But relative to its relationship to other disciplines, such as folklore or history, historical archaeology's reliance on the natural sciences is less than is that of prehistory. This lessened dependency on the natural sciences is but a reflection of the role played by the natural world in the history of human development. The earlier in time one goes, the more people were directly and intimately tied to their environment, so that such disciplines as paleontology and geology are essential to the proper understanding of life in the distant past. As culture became more complex, our removal from the natural world increased. Since historical archaeology treats only the past few hundred years of our multimillion-year history, it follows that this last, brief time would find us at our greatest remove.

The existence of artifacts and written records from the same society makes possible the use of historical archaeological materials for the testing and refinement of numerous methods and theories developed by prehistorians. An excellent example of such refinement is the use of New England colonial gravestone designs to observe stylistic change under conditions of rigorous control. This study, described fully in a later chapter in this book, not only confirmed in a positive fashion a dating technique—seriation—long a standby for prehistorians, but also showed how design changed for very specific cultural reasons. We have seen that probate inventories are among the most useful primary documents to the historical archaeologist. As documents for independent controlled checking of archaeological results they are excellent, since it is logical to assume that they should bear a close relation to that which is recovered from sites of the same period. On occasion they do not, but the disagreement only forces the archaeologist to ask more enlightened questions of his or her data. More often, the fit between archaeological collections and inventory materials is comfortable, and this in turn permits the archaeologist a greater assurance that the sample is somewhat representative.

On a more general level, the combined use of archaeological and documentary materials should permit us to say something about the past that could not have been said using only one set of data. This criterion is the most critical to be applied to avoid the charge often heard that historical archaeology is "an expensive way of learning what we already know." A simple example will make this clear. The existence of earthfast construction in the seventeenth- and earlier-eighteenth-century Chesapeake is known almost entirely through archaeological evidence. While there are occasional passing references to such construction in the documents, its widespread and sometimes universal use was only determined through the excavation of large numbers of sites in Maryland and Virginia. In an important study of this architectural tradition, Cary Carson and his colleagues have shown that this way of constructing a house is closely correlated with the cultivation of tobacco to the exclusion of other cash crops.[7] Throughout the region, in some places earlier and in others later, tobacco monoculture gave way to mixed crop farming, and when this occurred, more substantial permanent dwelling houses were built. The reasons for this relationship are clear. Tobacco cultivation is labor intensive in comparison to mixed crop farming. In a world of limited resources, cheap land, and expensive labor, one had to set priorities, and tobacco production took precedence over expensive housing. We could not have known this without the archaeology, which provided information on the distribution and date of houses built in the earthfast tradition, and without the documents, we would not have known the pattern of agricultural change. Taken together, the two sets of information not only allow us to say something about attitudes toward place and permanence, but also when these attitudes changed in different parts of the Chesapeake region.

Perhaps the most important and subtle aspects of the control afforded by historical archaeology are those factors that would be forever lost to the prehistorian but can be seen to have a strong effect on the nature of cultural change as reflected by the archaeological data. Such aspects of a past people as the way in which they perceived their environment, the worldview that underlay the organization of their physical universe, and the way ideology shaped their lives are as difficult to discover in prehistory as they are important. But in working in the context of historical material culture, the relationship between material culture and cognition begins to come into focus.[8]

Such insights call into sharp question some of the basic tenets of prehistoric archaeology: that culture is an adaptive device, so that to be successful, it tends to a close fit with the environment; that the simplest, most efficient explanation of archaeological data is most likely the correct one; and that we are rational beings, whose actions can be understood only in terms of common sense. What historical archaeology teaches us is that common sense is culturally relative, that in the past people have done things and behaved in ways that to us might seem almost irrational but that to them may not have been, and that the phenomenon of culture change is far more complex and imponderable than we might suspect were we to rely only on the detailing of it by prehistorians. The simple fact that the Shaker sect of nineteenth-century America controlled the shape, physical arrangement, and even the color of their furniture for strong religious reasons tells us that there are factors at work on the form and function of the artifacts of the past that are beyond recovery, either by logic, hypothesis and deduction, or endless guessing. They are available, however, to the historical archaeologist if intelligent and imaginative use is made of the rich supporting materials, and at least can serve as a suggestion of a more diverse set of factors than has been heretofore considered in prehistory.

So far, we have described some of the more important ways in which historical archaeology compares with prehistory. We must still consider one more aspect of historical

in small things forgotten

archaeology: the relationship it has to the study of material culture. Material culture, it is often correctly said, is not culture but its product. Culture is socially transmitted rules for behavior, ways of thinking about and doing things. We inherit our culture from the teachings and examples of our elders and our peers rather than from genes, whether it is the language we speak, the religious beliefs that we subscribe to, or the laws that govern our society. All such behavior is reflected in subtle and important ways in the manner in which we shape our physical world. Material culture is usually considered to be roughly synonymous with artifacts, the vast universe of objects used by humankind to cope with the physical world, to facilitate social intercourse, and to benefit our state of mind. A somewhat broader definition of material culture is useful in emphasizing how profoundly our world is the product of our thoughts, as *that sector of our physical environment that we modify through culturally determined behavior*. This definition includes all artifacts, from the simplest, such as a common pin, to the most complex, such as an interplanetary space vehicle. But the physical environment includes more than what most definitions of material culture recognize. We can also consider cuts of meat as material culture, since there are many ways to dress an animal; plowed fields; even the horse that pulls the plow, since scientific breeding of livestock involves the conscious modification of an animal's form according to culturally derived ideals. Our body itself is a part of our physical environment, so that such things as parades, dancing, and all aspects of kinesics—human motion—fit within our definition. Nor is the definition limited only to matter in the solid state. Fountains are liquid examples, as are lily ponds, and material that is partly gas includes hot-air balloons and neon signs. I have suggested in *Invitation to Archaeology*[9] that even language is a part of material culture, a prime example of it in its gaseous state. Words, after all, are air masses shaped by the speech apparatus according to culturally acquired rules.

The advantages of this general definition of material culture are twofold. First, since disciplines such as kinesics and linguistics have developed analytical techniques well suited to their subject matter, these techniques might well be of use to the student of material culture. Second, it forces us to look at archaeological information in the broader framework of whole material cultural systems, which might well permit sharper delineations of their corresponding behavioral systems. For example, we know from the study of proxemics, which deals with spatial relationships between people as they are dictated culturally, that all cultures have typical sets of "invisible" limits that dictate the placement of people in a social situation. We have all at some time or other encountered people who stood too close while talking; the resulting discomfort is due to the closeness violating our perception of the cultural rule that dictates a proper distance in such a situation. The same rules apply to the relationship, in a systemic way, between people and the architectural space they occupy. Thus any study of the size of rooms in an early American building must take into account this relationship, a subject

in small things forgotten

discussed by Glassie in his excellent work on Virginia folk housing.

Since historical archaeology must deal with not only excavated material from the American past but also all that has survived above the ground, including old houses, collections of pottery, weapons, bottles, glassware, cutlery, and textiles, it is truly the study of American material culture in historical perspective. It stands in contrast to the study of history or the decorative arts not so much in terms of subject matter as in terms of its analytical approach. An appreciation for the simple details of past existence, which escape historical mention, and for simple artifacts, not deemed significant in art-historical terms, viewed from the perspective of a broad social-scientific base, characterizes historical archaeology.

2

the anglo-american past

The personalities of prehistory will remain forever nameless and without faces. Dynamic and charismatic personae have peopled the stage of history: individuals such as the Paiute prophet Wovoka, who brought the Ghost Dance to the Plains Indians, George Washington, Susan B. Anthony, Phillis Wheatley, Stonewall Jackson, and many others of the American past. But in our not knowing them on personal, individual terms lies a great asset, for the true story of a people depends less on such knowledge than on a broader and more general familiarity with what life was like for all people.

However, there is often a tendency among historical archaeologists to excavate a site merely because some important person resided there. Such archaeology attracts the lay public's attention, and the news media give it good coverage. After all, history classes focus on the most powerful leader, the most significant event, or the key date. Robert E. Lee's command of the Army of Northern Virginia, and the fact that he suffered a disastrous defeat at Gettysburg, are generally known facts to most people; far fewer realize that the armies that faced each other in the July heat of southern Pennsylvania represented two strongly contrasting cultures. The South was the cultural heir of the Anglo-American tradition brought to America in the seventeenth century, culturally homogeneous and primarily agrarian in the ancient English tradition, while the North was culturally heterogeneous, a polyglot society that owed its form to the impact of the Industrial Revolution and the massive immigration from European nations it generated. These differences lay at the root of the economic and social differences that precipitated America's most bitter conflict.

To the historical archaeologist, such broad cultural contrasts and basic human motivations are of greater interest and significance than detailed specifics concerning discrete events or historical personages. It was an interest in such a personage that led James Hall to Duxbury, Massachusetts, in 1856. A civil engineer by profession, Hall was a descendant of Miles Standish, the military leader of the *Mayflower* Pilgrims who was immortalized by Henry Wadsworth Longfellow in the long narrative poem *The Courtship of Miles Standish*. The site of Standish's house was known and visible as a depression in the ground marking the location of an old, filled-in cellar. Standish had moved across the bay from Plymouth to Duxbury in 1629, as had John Alden, his supposed rival for the affections of Priscilla Mullins. This move was a part of the dispersal of the original fortified community of New Plimoth to the scattered farmsteads that would become typical of Plymouth Colony during the late seventeenth century. Hall conducted a dig of his illustrious ancestor's house, and his excavations were meticulous. As such, they stand as the earliest example of historic archaeology known, and possibly the first controlled excavation ever carried out.

The notes, map, and artifacts from this project came to light in 1963, when Hall's descendants discovered them among the effects of one of their number in Mexico. They were sent to the museum of the Pilgrim Society, in Plymouth, Massachusetts, where today they are a part of the collections. The map of the site is a credit to Hall's engineering expertise. He carefully created scale plans of the foundations he exposed. Extensive notes on the map refer to the stratigraphy of the site, and many of the artifacts are mapped in place. It is standard modern practice to relate excavations to a *datum point,* a fixed locus, on or near the site, that will not disappear through the years. The purpose of this practice is to insure that later excavators, should they desire to restudy the site, can easily locate the original diggings. Hall used not one but two datum points: springs in the near vicinity which are still flowing over a century later.

Most of the artifacts that Hall recovered have become lost over the years, but those that survive carry neat labels relating them to the map. The Miles Standish site thus stands as an important historical landmark not because it was Standish's house but because it marks an early episode in the development of archaeology, both historical and pre-historic.

The excavation of the Standish house site is probably unique in historical archaeology. But it is only one of a large number of sites dug for the simple reason that they were the homes of important persons. Mount Vernon and Monticello have been the scenes of excavations, as have been the homes of John Alden, Henry David Thoreau, and Benjamin Franklin. In some cases, the work has been done in conjunction with over-all restoration and interpretive programs on the historic site in question. But, even in such a situation, the reason for the selection of the site, whether for restoration or for archaeology for its own sake, is primarily that a person of note resided there. Not only does such archaeology make questions of general cultural significance secondary, but since most famous people were of the more elite sector of society, if we were to depend only on such data for our interpretation of the American past, the picture would be decidedly skewed in the direction of greater affluence and status.

The individual may be a source of problems in historic archaeology in yet another and very different way. Humans have a marvelous and endearing capacity to indulge in whimsey, often realizing our ideas by the creation of incredible edifices. The Watts Towers in downtown Los Angeles are only one example of such creations. What has this to do with archaeology? Perhaps little, but one can but wonder if certain "mysterious" ruins on the American landscape might be attributed to similar motivations. Tucson, Arizona, is the site of "The Valley of the Moon," an amazing complex of underground tunnels, rooms, and reflecting pools, with miniature buildings here and there containing dioramas from fairy tales. Abandoned today, it was the work of one man, created for the entertainment of the people of Tucson in the 1930s. The facts in this case are well known. However, in New Salem, New Hampshire, there is a complex of stone ruins known as "Mystery Hill," which has been the center of considerable controversy for years. These stone rooms, tunnels, and walls have been variously interpreted as root cellars; the excavation residue from the mining of raw materials for a seventeenth-century ironworks in Saugus, Massachusetts; a megalithic structure built by Irish monks or even by the carriers of the megalithic culture of Neolithic Europe in the third millennium B.C. Yet, one piece of historical information provides the necessary clue to the true meaning of Mystery Hill. In the 1920s, a wealthy individual set about to "restore" certain stone structures on the site. He was convinced that an order of Irish monks had come to New England in the ninth century, and saw the site as evidence of their presence. We know that he had at his disposal a team of oxen and a crew of laborers and more than sufficient capital to carry out the restoration. Yet no one knows how much "new" construction was involved in this project.

The similarities between Mystery Hill and The Valley of the Moon seem more than coincidental; since the facts of the creation of the latter are better known, one naturally wonders about the former. If any lesson is to be learned

in small things forgotten

from these examples, it is that due allowance must be made for the totally idiosyncratic and occasionally eccentric behavior of certain people, now and in the past.

This brief discussion of "individual archaeology" should serve as a *caveat* that some thought must be given to the questions the historical archaeologist should seek to answer in his work. All archaeologists who are at work today agree that some intelligent research design should underlie their studies, and that it should be spelled out in some detail before the first shovelful of sod is removed from a site.

The total number of historical archaeological sites in eastern North America alone must be astronomical. In contrast to prehistoric sites, which are the result of a population thinly dispersed across the American landscape and which form a very valuable and scarce resource, historical sites, since they represent the period of maximum population in America, increase in number and complexity over time at a spectacular rate. Every house is a part of a site that surrounds it, as is every public building, barn, or factory. With such a superabundance of material with which to work, the historical archaeologist must give explicit and careful thought to the reasons for digging this site now, that one later, and yet another in the distant future.

Of course, if the archaeologists' research design is too narrowly or rigidly constructed, there is no guarantee that its requirements will be satisfied by any given site's yield of data. The trick is to test, through archaeology, certain assumptions that are sufficiently general on the one hand to hold promise of refutation or support from adequate information, but are on the other hand specific enough to assure a more detailed knowledge of the past as a result. Indeed, it is far more important that archaeologists be sensitive to questions of general cultural significance that they can apply to the data if they seem appropriate than to be locked into a single restricted approach. There are too many interested parties involved in historical archaeology and its related disciplines, representing different but valid viewpoints, to permit one's research strategy to derive from only one. In the case of salvage archaeology, involving the excavation of sites threatened by destruction from one or another agency, it is often impossible to construct a research design that is wholly appropriate without forcing the fit between data and design. Yet, in doing such archaeology, more often than not new and useful information, which can be placed in the context of broad and current social-scientific thought, is forthcoming, even though it was not explicitly being sought before the fact of excavation. A good example of such salvage work is provided by the excavation of a late-seventeenth-century tavern on Cape Cod.

Great Island forms the western side of Wellfleet Bay, on the outer Cape. No longer an island, but connected to the mainland by a narrow sand bar, it is a part of the Cape Cod National Seashore. For years, local tradition had it that one Samuel Smith had operated a tavern on the island in the late-seventeenth century. An archaeological site atop a high bluff was thought by many to be the remains of Smith's tavern. Other traditions held that the site had been

in small things forgotten

a Dutch trading post established in the early 1600s. The site had been dug into by unauthorized parties over the years, and the National Park Service decided to have it properly studied before any further damage was done to it.

What came to light was the well-preserved foundation of a large building with a floor plan typical of New England "salt box" construction. Fifty feet long and thirty feet wide, it had a central chimney and two large, flanking rooms and a lean-to at the rear. The artifacts the excavations produced numbered in the tens of thousands: pottery, window glass, parts of wine bottles and glasses, clay pipe-stems and bowls, nails, hinges, buckles, buttons, spoons, and forks—a rich and representative selection of domestic materials. They amply demonstrated that the site was English and dated from circa 1690 to about 1740, supporting the tradition of Smith's tavern and laying to rest the site's identification with Dutch traders earlier in the seventeenth century.

The resolution of one question raised another. Since Great Island was separated from the mainland during the time the tavern was in use, its location seemed somewhat remote for patrons, who would have had to come by boat from Wellfleet and other neighboring communities. What special function might the tavern have served that would explain its location? Its identification as a tavern, rather than as a simple dwelling house, was supported by its large size and very great numbers of fragments of clay pipes and utensils for eating and drinking. Each of the main rooms had a cellar beneath its floor. One was filled with clean sand, but on its floor was found a chopping block made from the cervical vertebra of a large whale. The other cellar was filled with refuse and included quantities of whalebone and the foreshaft of a harpoon.

These discoveries made sense in the light of the recorded history of Wellfleet and other outer Cape Cod towns. This area saw the earliest whaling by English colonists in New England. A Cape Cod whaler, Ichabod Paddock, is credited with introducing whaling to Nantucket Island in 1690, and New Bedford did not become a whaling center until the end of the eighteenth century. The whale commonly hunted on Cape Cod was the blackfish, a small animal that could be hunted from shore in small boats or driven ashore and killed. In 1793 a writer described what he knew of earlier Wellfleet whaling practices: "When they [the blackfish] come within our harbor, boats surround them. They are as easily driven to the shore as cattle or sheep are driven on land. The tide leaves them and they are easily killed. They are a fish of the whale kind, and will average a barrel of oil each. I have seen nearly four hundred at one time lying dead on the shore." Great Island occupies a commanding position in Wellfleet's harbor, and the location of the tavern, atop a high bluff, would have afforded a superb lookout for schools of blackfish. A tavern in such a location would have served as a center for the shore whalers, a place to which to repair nearby when there were no whales to be hunted.

Further support to this interpretation of the site comes

from the time of its occupation. The period 1690–1740 is indicated by pipestem dates as well as ceramic evidence. Frechen stoneware, from Germany, a brown, mottled, salt-glazed pottery commonly made in the form of jugs with grotesque faces molded on their shoulders, dates at the latest to the end of the seventeenth century. Small quantities of this pottery were recovered. A *terminus ante quem* of 1740 is suggested by the total absence of a distinctive English-made white stoneware from the Staffordshire district that is very common on sites occupied after this date Again, certain key documents fit with the archaeological information and lend further support to this date. The writer quoted above remarked at the same time: "It is not, however, very often of late that these fish come into our harbor." In the March 20, 1727, issue of the Boston *News Letter* we read: "We hear from towns on the Cape that the whale fishery among them has failed much this winter, as it has done for several winters past, but having found out the way of going to sea upon that business . . . they are now fitting out several vessels to sail with all expedition upon that dangerous design this spring . . ."

The whalebone in the site, its identification as a tavern, its period of occupation, and the accounts of a contemporary newspaper and a diarist all fit comfortably to demonstrate that the tavern, accommodating shore whalers in the early eighteenth century, had no further purpose once the blackfish no longer came near the shore with regularity and dependability. What could not have been determined solely from the documentary sources was the existence of such a specialized, occupation-related establishment, or its role in the Wellfleet whale fisheries.

This example again shows the way in which written and archaeological information can combine to give a more detailed picture than either could separately. The Great Island site was dug only because it was in danger of destruction, but the illumination in greater detail of a subsistence and economic process would be sufficient justification for having done the work. Yet other materials recovered from the site are of interest to scholars in other disciplines as well. Impressions of building laths in hundreds of plaster fragments from the building's walls showed that the siding of the building had been large sawn planks attached to the frame vertically. This method of siding, according to architectural historians studying early New England building, is typical of Plymouth Colony architecture, and its existence at Wellfleet extended the known range of the technique well out onto Cape Cod. In fact, so few seventeenth-century buildings have survived in southeastern Massachusetts that the addition of this example was a truly major and significant one. This information is also not without broader cultural implications, since a more detailed knowledge of regional variation in architectural forms allows us to make better sense out of the manner in which the English building tradition was altered and diversified regionally in the New World. The architectural information is of value to architectural historians and folklorists who study early building forms; the rich variety of artifacts, to students of ceramic history and the decorative arts; and the elucidation of the tavern's role in the whaling industry, to workers in local history detailing Cape Cod's past.

Of course, there are also those instances when archaeological research can enjoy the luxury of being conducted in the absence of salvage constraints; research designs can be carefully developed and refined over time. Among others, the archaeological programs at Colonial Williamsburg, Historic Annapolis, Old Sturbridge Village, and Monticello have been in existence for years, and have been conducted for the most part at a relatively unhurried pace. We can consider one such program in greater detail, to see how a single project can grow and develop over the years.

Flowerdew Hundred,[1] Virginia, is a working farm located on the south side of the James River roughly halfway between Richmond and Williamsburg. Included within its boundaries is the thousand-acre tract granted to George Yeardley, first royal governor of Virginia, in 1619, and possibly even earlier. It has been continuously occupied from the early seventeenth century through the twentieth, and since there has been no development of the property of a residential or industrial nature, site preservation is excellent. Painstaking surveys of surface evidence of past occupations, carried out in the spring when the plows have turned the earth and rain has washed artifacts clean of soil, have produced more than a hundred sites representing human occupation from as early as 10,000 B.C. through the later nineteenth century. Furthermore, almost all of the sites dating to the historic period represent relatively brief occupations, of the order of a generation or so, providing the archaeologist with a perfect context in which to observe change in material culture over time, and to determine what these changes mean in more general cultural historical terms.

Archaeological investigations have been under way at Flowerdew Hundred since 1971, encouraged and supported to a large extent by the present owner, David A. Harrison III, whose interest in the history of his farm was aroused shortly after he acquired the property in 1969. The results of this research have been spectacular, allowing us to see how the development of an early English colonial culture was played out in one location, to become something distinctively American, and ultimately modern. The documentary record for Flowerdew Hundred is rather thin. The county in which it is located, Prince George, lost many of its records to fire during the Civil War. However, we do have a relatively clear picture of the succession of owners of the property over time. The entire thousand acres initially owned by Yeardley were conveyed to Abraham Piersey in 1624, who on his death in 1628 passed the property to his daughter Elizabeth. She in turn sold it to a local merchant, William Barker, who willed it to his son John. Upon John's death, the property passed to his two sisters in 1673, from which time the property underwent successive subdivision, with the maximum number of owners residing on smaller landholdings occurring during the first quarter of the eighteenth century. But by mid-century, the land was being

in small things forgotten

assembled in increasingly larger tracts, with fewer owners, and by the early nineteenth century, under the ownership of John Vaughn Willcox, it was once again consolidated into the thousand-acre plantation first granted to Yeardley in 1619. It has remained a single tract since that time.

There is no question of the value of such information; in fact, it is of more than passing interest that almost all land conveyances were along lines of blood relationships. But useful as this knowledge is, it falls short of the more important question, of how all of these people passed their lives. What did living at Flowerdew Hundred actually mean to these people? How did they live out their days, and what were their ties to the larger world of colonial Virginia and America? The records are largely silent on these matters, but archaeology has provided some important answers.

The first excavations at Flowerdew Hundred were carried out when historical archaeology was just emerging as a distinct field of inquiry, and understandably, there was great interest in the physical form of the first English settlements in America. Jamestown's original fort was thought to have been eroded away by the James River, which we now know not to have been the case,[2] and no one had seen a site from the first two decades of the struggling colony's existence. Seven years of painstaking fieldwork revealed the physical remains of Yeardley's first settlement, consisting of several dwelling houses, a fortified compound, and a defensive redoubt.[3] In these features, the settlement was similar to those established by the English in Ulster only a few years earlier, and the same layout was to be found later at Martin's Hundred, another early settlement farther down the James River below Jamestown.[4] The Yeardley settlement lies at the northern end of the property, but there are other sites from the same time located along a north-south line to the southern end, almost as if they had been connected by a road of some type. While we will probably never know the names of the people who occupied these sites, archaeology has shown us how they lived. But such knowledge was not immediately forthcoming; it had to await new scholarship and further archaeology at Flowerdew Hundred. By 1980, the scope of archaeological excavations was expanded to include sites from the eighteenth and nineteenth centuries, in an attempt to secure a greater temporal perspective on events on the plantation. By 1984, excavation and intensive surface survey had produced large collections from twenty sites on the property, and it was these collections that provided the data which were used to construct an overall research design which has guided the archaeological program in the years since.

As is so often the case, the initial phase of the development of the research program was the result of almost serendipitous events. In the course of organizing the materials from seventeen of the sites located on the fertile flood plain, pipe stem histograms were prepared for each site that produced stems in sufficient quantity to provide reasonably dependable results. When these histograms were compared, a pattern emerged that no one had expected. The sites fell

in small things forgotten

into three distinct groups, those in each showing an almost identical pattern, and each differing clearly from the other two. The earliest group of sites showed a sharp peak in their histograms, indicating a rather short occupation between 1619 and 1660, following which they appear to have been abandoned. The second group of sites shared in a much flatter histogram pattern, indicating longer occupation, between circa 1630 and 1700, and overlapping those histograms from the sites in both the first and third groups. The final group of sites showed a shorter period of occupation once more, between circa 1700 and 1750. The end of this last occupation appears to have resulted from people moving away from the river bottom to a ridge to the west. Clearly, such a pattern of settlement history must be the result of more than random happenings, and those events and forces which shaped the lives of Flowerdew Hundred's residents were probably of more than local significance. Turning to the broader canvas of Virginia history of which Flowerdew Hundred was but a small but significant part, we can see three aspects of that history which might well account for the pattern seen at the local level, these being the tobacco boom of the earlier seventeenth century, the attempt by the colonies to become economically independent of the mother country during the middle to late seventeenth century, and the dramatic increase in the importation of African slaves in the early years of the eighteenth century. While these connections were put forth only tentatively at first, corroboration from the archaeological evidence made the relationship far more likely. The same pattern has subsequently been found at Martin's Hundred, lending even more credibility to the explanation.

John Rolfe's introduction of a high-quality strain of tobacco from Trinidad in 1616 set Virginia's economy on a narrow but lucrative course. The years before had been marked by discontent and disaster, but the new crop changed all of this. Those who survived the "seasoning" of Virginia's fever-ridden summers could hope to amass a fortune, and with luck, return to England wealthy enough to establish a fine estate and provide for their children a leisurely and comfortable life. Tobacco remained king through the mid seventeenth century, and as we have seen, tobacco planters' priorities were such that most chose to put the bulk of their capital into producing a lucrative crop, with substantial house construction relegated to secondary importance. This state of affairs lasted through the 1660s, to be followed by a sharp decline in tobacco prices, making its cultivation a much less attractive proposition than it had been during the years of the tobacco boom.

But while most Virginians were deeply committed to the production of tobacco, there were some who looked to other sources of income, beginning in the early years of the colony. Between the 1630s and the 1660s various types of local industry were being developed in an attempt to gain some economic independence from England, if not complete self-sufficiency. By mid-century a variety of domestically produced goods made their appearance, including leather and leather products, smelted iron, smoking pipes,

in small things forgotten

ceramics, and even ships. Such domestic industrial production was seen by England not to be in its best interests, and after the passage of the Navigation Acts in 1651 and 1660, which restricted colonial trade to only English goods, transported on English ships, Parliament followed with formal legislation forbidding local production of needed commodities. At the same time, the Virginia assembly was promoting local production through legislation of its own. During the last quarter century, following Bacon's Rebellion, local production slowed almost to a halt, brought about by even more aggressive action by the Crown. It was, as one writer has said, "the end of American independence."

But by century's end, other forces were at work which reshaped the Virginia economy once again. Inexpensive labor, in the form of slaves brought from Africa, made the production of tobacco a paying proposition once more. While there had been a small number of Africans in the colony from its early years, this number increased dramatically in the years following 1680, and by the turn of the century as many as six thousand slaves were in Virginia, where before there had been only hundreds.

The timing of these three episodes in seventeenth-century Virginia history fits comfortably with the dates of occupation of the three groups of sites at Flowerdew Hundred, and at Martin's Hundred as well. The earliest group might be of those sites occupied during the tobacco boom and abandoned at its close; the second group could relate in some way to local industrial production, and the third, to the emergence of large-scale slavery in the colony. It remained to examine the archaeological evidence to determine if these relationships were truly causal and therefore valid. Of course, final and conclusive results must await the excavation of all seventeen sites in question, but those which have been excavated to date, and the material in surface collections from those which have not, all support and illuminate this explanation of Flowerdew Hundred's settlement history. And, as with all properly constructed research designs, this one permits the formulation of questions to be tested against the material recovered from the ground.

Three of the seven sites in the first group have been excavated, and all three have buildings that were constructed in the earthfast tradition. The remaining four have been plowed for decades, and no evidence of more substantial construction, such as brick footings or massive hearths, has come to light. While earthfast construction continued at Flowerdew Hundred into the first half of the eighteenth century, the two sites from the second group which have been excavated revealed the remains of buildings built in a different style, one suggesting a stronger commitment to place, a greater sense of permanence. The first of these is somewhat ambiguous in form, with a very large cellar, paved with square tiles, and no evidence of posts which would have supported the frame. Fragments of malformed smoking pipes known as wasters were recovered, suggesting that pipe production was carried out at the site. This site may have been that of the home of William Barker, who, as a merchant, would have had an interest in producing commodities for sale. The second site produced evidence of both local industry and more substantial architecture. The dwelling house had been constructed by setting posts inside a large cellar, woodlined and with a cross partition. A space between the walls and the outside of the cellar pit seems to have been intended for some kind of facing, perhaps of brick, very reminiscent of the house described in a building contract from Ipswich, Massachusetts, dating to 1638.[5] Outside the house there were series of pits which have been interpreted as relating to the production of bog iron, a simple household industry, manageable by just a few people, but producing a reasonable quantity of usable metal.[6] All of the sites from the third group, dating primarily to the first half of the eighteenth century, have produced, either from excavation or surface finds, quantities of a kind of ceramic known as Colono ware.[7] None of the sites in the other groups have yielded this type of pottery. Unglazed, handmade, and fired at a low temperature, Colono ware is believed to have been made by slaves, lending credence to the relationship between these sites and the appearance of large-scale slavery at the time.

The likely relationship between the settlement history at Flowerdew Hundred and events taking place in the larger world permits us to say something about the way in which the lives of the plantation's inhabitants were shaped and given direction. The occupants of the sites of the first group were "tobacco boomers," and while we know that they abandoned their homesteads in the 1660s, we will never know where they went, or for that matter, who they were. But we do know something about their way of life, their attitudes, and their priorities. Likewise with the inhabitants of the sites of group two. They appear to have had a different outlook on life, a stronger sense of place and belonging, and pursued different economic goals. The people who lived on the sites of the third group in all likelihood represent the very beginnings of what would become the slaveholding agrarian elite of eighteenth-century Virginia, people like William Byrd, Landon Carter, and Carter Burwell. Archaeology and the written record were critical to this explanation; it could not have been arrived at without a combination of both.

The tiny ships that crossed the Atlantic in the early seventeenth century, vessels such as the *Susan Constant,* the *Mayflower,* the *Ark,* the *Dove,* and the *Arabella,* all carried a precious cargo. Their passengers, English emigrants who had come to the New World for a variety of reasons, brought with them a blueprint—in their minds—for recreating the culture they had left behind. Likewise, the unwilling passengers aboard the thousands of slave ships that made the same crossing brought with them, against enormous odds, traditions from their West African homelands which would endure in a new and hostile environment. Both would come together in the New World, and combine in complex ways through both resistance and accommodation to form a new culture, one not seen before and one that would become a vital component of our modern society. For the English, theirs was a tradition that owed much of its form to the English Middle Ages, recently drawn to a close. The Renaissance, which revolutionized our view of ourselves and our world, had not yet made its impact on the simple people of England, and it would be more than a century before its effects could be measured among their counterparts in North America.

Until circa 1660, Anglo-American colonial culture was essentially that of old England, since the first native-born generation was still a minority of younger people. The first four decades undoubtedly saw the establishment of the rural English tradition on New World soil. There were differences: the colonies were not established by members of the elite, and there was a resultant skew in cultural form in the direction of that of simple husbandmen and yeomen. Governor William Bradford of Plymouth wrote in his history of the colony: ". . . they [the Plymouth colonists] were not acquainted with trades nor traffic . . . but had only been used to a plain country life and the innocent trade of husbandry."[8] Other differences appear between English and American cultures at this time, but they are slight in comparison to the similarity. English common law controlled the society; the religion, even of those dissenting from the established church, was English, as was the entire material culture. Even "the first Thanksgiving," which we observe today in a much altered form, was a reenactment of the English harvest home, a tradition of great antiquity in the home country.[9] The essentially agrarian nature of the culture of America's English settlers is important to keep in mind when we seek comparisons with English architectural forms, ways of cooking and eating food, and other archaeologically available information. The best fit should be found in the culture of the English yeoman.

The year 1660 marked the restoration of the Crown in England under Charles II, and with it came a renewed interest in the American colonies. They had existed in considerable isolation before that time, enforced by the success of the Puritan revolution, which removed one of the strong motivations for removal to the New World. The time before 1660 saw the beginning of a drift away from the parent culture by American colonists, even though distinctive cultural differences would not be expected until a substantial population of people who had never seen England had developed. Of course, some immigration continued throughout, and colonial trade slowly increased.

The course of cultural development from 1680 until circa 1760 can be illustrated by an analogy with a rocket, fired into the atmosphere, that does not achieve escape velocity. Such a missile travels at its greatest speed immediately after firing, and while moving farther from the earth's surface, moves increasingly slower, until it stops rising and returns to earth, accelerating at a rate equal to its upward deceleration. Likewise did American colonial culture move away from its English parent beginning sometime prior to 1660, but while still diverging as the seventeenth century wore on, it did so at an increasingly slower rate, until it was brought back into the domain of English culture a second time, around the middle of the eighteenth century. This

in small things forgotten

"re-Anglicization" of American culture meant that on the eve of the American Revolution, Americans were more English than they had been in the past since the first years of the colonies.

During this century-long second phase in Anglo-American history, strong traditional cultures developed, with great regional diversity. They were folk cultures, changing slowly, and interacting with their neighbors to a very limited degree. Such isolation was certainly reinforced by poor transportation and communication facilities at the time, and by strong, locally oriented political units. We shall see later that archaeological research confirms this diversity and cultural conservatism in striking fashion.

Such traditional societies are termed *peasant societies* by anthropologists. Peasants the world over share in a common culture. Workers of the land, they exist in relation to and provide support for urban centers. Their values are conservative and traditional, characterized by close ties to kin; suspicion of outsiders, change, or innovation; and a life governed by the change of seasons. Our concern here is with the culture of the rural peoples of colonial America at the time, and it is these people who were most typical of peasant culture. The cities during this period—Portsmouth, Boston, Newport, New York, Philadelphia, and Charleston—had their merchants, their religious and political leaders, and their social elite, but they should not be thought of as typical of English colonial culture. Rather, it is the rural tiller of the land, who lived in hundreds of tiny communities, who made the cities possible and represents the true character of colonial Anglo-America. The cosmopolitan city dwellers were an important quantity, however, in the cultural transformations that took place in the seventeenth and eighteenth centuries. We can see them as brokers of taste and fashion. It was they who sent their sons to England to study architecture, who wanted the latest styles of clothing, china, and furniture. The cultural changes that mark the beginning of the third period, in about 1760, had their origins in the urban centers, where they had appeared as much as a half century or more earlier.

What are these changes? The full re-entry of the American colonies into the English cultural sphere during the eighteenth century involved an English culture profoundly changed from its early-seventeenth-century form. Before 1650 the impact of the Renaissance on the material culture of England was to be seen in little more than a handful of buildings designed by Inigo Jones, an architect familiar with the work of Andrea Palladio, the great Italian architect whose *Four Books of Architecture* was the chief instrument by which Renaissance design was introduced to the Anglo-American world. A century later, the Renaissance influence on English material culture was profound, and one might surmise that this influence went far beyond only the material, and in subtle ways had reformed the English worldview into something totally different from its earlier, medieval form. We might call this new worldview *Georgian,* a term that in its specific sense designates the architectural style that most typifies Anglo-American Renaissance building.

in small things forgotten

This contrast between the Georgian and the medieval worldview(s) has been commented upon by scholars in various disciplines. The art historian Alan Gowans remarks:

> More than a change of style or detail is involved here: it is a change in basic tradition. Like folk buildings earlier, these structures grow out of a way of life, a new and different concept of the relationship between man and nature. Gone is the medieval "acceptance" of nature taking its course, along with the unworked materials, exposed construction, and additive composition that expressed it. This design is informed by very different convictions: that the world has a basic immutable order; that men by powers of reason can discover what that order is; and that, discovering it, they can control environment as they will.[10]

Order and control: the eighteenth century is called the age of reason, and it saw the rise of scientific thought in the Western world and the development of Renaissance-derived form, balanced and ordered, in the Anglo-American world. By 1760 significant numbers of American colonists partook of this new worldview. Mechanical where the older was organic, balanced where the older had been asymmetrical, individualized where the older had been corporate, this new way of perceiving the world is the hallmark of our third period, which lasts to the present and accounts for much of the way in which we ourselves look out upon reality.

The archaeological concepts of *horizon* and *tradition* are made explicit by the differences between the first two periods and the third. An archaeological tradition as it is defined in prehistory is a pattern of long persistence of cultural traits in a restricted geographical area. It is the hallmark of cultural conservatism, and examples of such traditions are many. Black-and-white-painted pottery, underground ceremonial chambers, and masonry dwellings are characteristic of a few cultures in the Four Corners area of the American Southwest for several centuries. Such traditions not only suggest a strong degree of conservatism but a stable pattern of permanent settlement, allowing such development to take place relatively undisturbed. In contrast, a horizon in archaeology is a pattern characterized by widespread distribution of a complex of cultural traits that lasts a relatively short time. Factors that might create the pattern of a horizon would include rapid military conquest or effective religious mission. Examples from prehistory include the distribution of artifacts typical of the Inca in Peru, widely spread as a result of that people's known efficiency in conquest and empire-building. Deeper in the past, the occurrence of distinctive tomb types, pottery design, and metal artifacts in the Mediterranean basin and beyond into the North Sea in the third millennium B.C. is usually interpreted as evidence of a largely sea-borne religious proselytization.

These archaeological concepts have their counterpart

in small things forgotten

in folklore as folk culture and popular culture. Folk culture is traditional and conservative; it exhibits great variation in space and relatively little change over time. Popular culture changes rapidly in time and shows great similarity over large areas. A good example of this contrast can be seen in the way in which the banjo is played. An African American musical instrument that was closely adapted to Anglo-American music in the highland South in the nineteenth century, the banjo is played by traditional musicians using two fingers in a variety of ways. At least three distinct two-finger playing techniques can be found along a line running from eastern Kentucky through western Virginia into North Carolina.[11] These styles are of considerable antiquity in their respective areas. Three-finger picking—the hallmark of bluegrass music—is a twentieth-century invention, and bluegrass musicians have played the banjo almost identically over the entire South, and well beyond. The three-finger technique has undergone a rather rapid evolution in the brief time it has been popular. This type of music is essentially urban, not rural, and thus is subject to the kinds of influences that are conducive to rapid change and dissemination.

We can see that the first two periods are times of folk culture that might appear as traditions were they to be examined archaeologically. The advent of popular culture occurs sometime during the third period, and the first horizon in Anglo-American archaeology might be expected to appear toward the end of the eighteenth century. The archaeological and material culture evidence demonstrates

Figure 2a. Georgian house

this, as we shall see. While we have developed a threefold division of the cultural development of Anglo-America, the major division occurs at the point of separation between the latter two periods. The ordered view of the world and people's place within it emerges at this time. Henry Glassie's analysis of folk material culture[12] shows that the Georgian worldview manifests itself in material culture in a bilaterally symmetrical, three-part format. This form is apparent in the architectural style that gives it its name. A Georgian house is rigorously symmetrical, and left and right halves are appended to a central element that shares its design form with the lateral ones but is also somewhat different (see Figure 2a). The contrast with a pre-Georgian, medievally derived house facade is striking, and the essentially organic form of the latter is manifest (see Figure 2b).

in small things forgotten

Figure 2b. The Mott farmhouse, Portsmouth, Rhode Island

But this structured worldview has impact far beyond architectural forms, and the extent to which it does demonstrates the power with which cognition reshaped the Anglo-American material world, beginning in the late eighteenth century.

Another expression of this new order is a strong emphasis on individuals and their place within their culture. The corporate nature of the earlier tradition extended to the organization of living space, of food consumption, and even of burial practices. We must look then at archaeological materials of the late eighteenth century for evidence of a new importance of the individual, and ways in which artifacts show this.

3

all the earthenware
plain and flowered

Classical Greek vases, crude earthenware, jars from Prehistoric Europe, Ancient Peruvian effigy vessels, fine Ming Dynasty porcelains and modern table settings of Spode or Wedgwood all reflect the great variety of the potter's craft, produced for thousands of years. The archaeologist attaches great importance to pottery, since ceramics is among the most informative kinds of material culture, in history and prehistory as well. Pottery is fragile yet indestructible: while it breaks easily, the fragments are highly resistant to corrosion and discoloration. It surprises many people on their first historical dig to unearth a piece of blue-and-gray German stoneware that looks as though it had been buried an hour earlier rather than some two centuries ago. The perishability of pottery when a part of the living world, and its longevity in the earth, means that the chances are good that any given piece was broken not a very long time after its manufacture, and that the archaeologist recovers large

3

collections of ceramic materials that have a high degree of chronological precision. Pottery is largely utilitarian. Its interpretation relates to the everyday aspects of past life rather than the more esoteric. Small wonder that the analysis of ceramics sometimes occupies what might at first seem a disproportionate amount of the archaeologist's attention and time.

Let us see what the pottery of Anglo-America can tell us about the development of its culture. The excavation of archaeological sites along the eastern seaboard ranging in date from circa 1610 through the mid nineteenth century has produced a vast ceramic collection representing virtually every type known to have occurred in the Anglo-American world during this time. These types are quite diverse, and volumes have been written on their history and identification.[1] We can consider them only in summary fashion, to show how they help us to understand Anglo-American cultural history.

Three general classes of pottery occur on historic sites in Anglo-America. *Earthenware* has a soft, water-absorbent body made impermeable by glazing. Such glaze is usually composed of lead sulfide or lead oxide, with additives to impart color or opacity, since a pure-lead glaze is colorless and transparent. *Stoneware* is a hard-bodied pottery that does not absorb water. Stoneware vessels need no glaze to make them impermeable, but a salt glaze was usually applied to them. Such glazing produced a smoother, more glassy surface, certainly easier to keep clean and probably more pleasing aesthetically. *Porcelain* is a highly vitrified

all the earthenware   69 white ceramic made from a special clay—kaolin—and is hard and impermeable to water. Unlike stoneware and earthenware, it is translucent. All three classes of ceramics occur on historic sites. From their abundance or rarity, their place of manufacture, and the purposes they served, we can discern much about the life and times of their owners.

Earthenwares were produced in England for millennia before the postmedieval period, and their manufacture by colonists began in America in the 1620s. Throughout the seventeenth and eighteenth centuries, the most common Anglo-American earthenware was an undecorated utility pottery with a buff or red body covered with a transparent lead glaze in colors ranging from yellow through green. Less common were decorated earthenwares. The decoration was often achieved through various uses of slip, white pipe clay applied in liquid form beneath the transparent glaze by trailing it on much in the manner of decorating a cake, or covering the entire body with it and then applying colors atop it or cutting through it to expose the contrasting color of the body beneath. These decorated ceramics, appropriately termed slipwares, were made in England from the early seventeenth century through the later eighteenth, and were joined by similar wares made in America from the later seventeenth century on. During the second half of the eighteenth century, English potters, particularly those of the important Staffordshire district, refined their wares. Pottery became thinner and harder, and the body color was lightened to nearly white. Lead glazes that earlier had had a yellow color due to impurities were purified and made nearly colorless. After 1750 these improvements led to Whieldon ware, with a light buff body and a mottled, multicolored glaze; to creamware in the 1760s, with an off-white body covered with an ivory-colored glaze; to pearlware in the 1770s, with a white body and a glaze whitened by the addition of cobalt (an effect similar to that obtained from laundry bluing); and finally in the 1830s, to white-bodied pottery with a colorless glaze of the type we find on our tables today.

The addition of tin oxide to a lead glaze results in an opaque white enamel. Tin glazing, as this process is called, is the hallmark of a second, parallel development of earthenware. Production of this kind of pottery began in England late in the sixteenth century and was derived from the production of similar pottery in the Low Countries, France, Spain, and Italy. Depending mainly on the nation where it is produced, such pottery is called majolica, faïence, and in its English and Dutch form, delft. Delftware is a common pottery of the entirety of the seventeenth and eighteenth centuries, although its popularity was gradually eclipsed by that of the inexpensive creamwares and pearlwares at the end of this period. It has a soft body, and the thick white glaze that covers it is painted in either blue or polychrome designs.

In Europe, stoneware production began in the North, and by the beginning of the seventeenth century such cities as Siegburg and Cologne were important centers of its production. Throughout the seventeenth century, two main types of Rhenish stoneware, as this class is called, were exported to England and subsequently to America. One, a brown ware, often in the form of bottles with a grotesque face molded on the shoulder, is typical of the seventeenth century (see Figure 3b). A blue-and-gray stoneware was also produced, in the Westerwald district of Germany, during the seventeenth and most of the eighteenth centuries. English production of stoneware began in the 1670s. At first it was mostly brown in color, but, by the 1720s, white stonewares, which by mid-century had reached a high level of technical refinement, had become common. At times, these white stonewares were decorated with blue designs. English stonewares had largely disappeared from the scene by the end of the eighteenth century; like delftware, they had been replaced by creamwares and pearlwares. Americans were producing stoneware in Virginia and Pennsylvania in the early eighteenth century. This production continued even after English stoneware manufacture had essentially ceased. Common late-nineteenth-century American stoneware is of the type seen in almost every antique store and flea market in the United States, jugs with freely painted cobalt-blue birds or flowers and the maker's name stamped in the shoulder.

On archaeological sites of people of modest means, porcelain is relatively uncommon. Most that is recovered is from China, where it was invented. It is usually decorated in blue designs on a natural white background, but often one can find polychrome-decorated pieces.

As one looks at the neatly sorted piles of potsherds in

an archaeological laboratory, it is difficult to picture the whole pieces they represent in a living context. A baby plays with a bowl of food on the floor; her father drinks ale from a stoneware mug while her mother removes an earthenware pot from the fire, where it has been simmering a pottage. On the cupboard are proudly displayed two large blue-and-white delft plates, one badly chipped. Outside, the chickens drink from a shallow earthenware milk pan. As with all artifacts, ceramics are a part of a living totality, and they must be understood in their functional and symbolic role.

The major role of ceramics in early America was in the foodways of the people. Foodways is a term used by the folklorist Jay Anderson to describe "the whole interrelated system of food conceptualization, procurement, distribution, preservation, preparation, and consumption shared by all members of a particular group."[2] Since ceramics played an important role in the foodways of Anglo-Americans, when these change, we might expect a change in the pattern of ceramic use. Their presence in the foodways complex in turn is dictated by four factors: availability, need, function, and social status.

In the early years of the seventeenth century, colonial Americans were dependent on England for their every need. Until local crafts and industries became established, the problem of availability was a very real one. Ceramics are fragile, and probably few were brought with the colonists among their personal equipment. Ceramics are omitted entirely from the many lists published as broadsides in seventeenth-century England telling settlers what equipment should be brought to the New World. Until the ceramic industry in America had become firmly established, it is certain that the amount of pottery a family owned depended on its availability from an uncertain supply line stretching some three thousand miles across the Atlantic.

If every kind of pottery made were easily available, a household would select only certain types, since their choice obviously would be dictated by need. This need in turn is an obvious function of the uses to which pottery might be put, and what other kinds of artifacts might serve the same purpose. Functionally equivalent artifacts in other materials such as wood or pewter might make unnecessary the adoption of certain ceramic forms.

Function is closely related to need, since it is the specific function of any artifact that, when unfulfilled, creates the need. Function is far more than a matter of technological efficiency. Lewis Binford has suggested three levels of function, and each applies to a different aspect of a people's behavior.[3] *Technomic function* is strictly utilitarian and relates directly to the technology of a culture. A candle used for lighting serves a technomic purpose, since it solves a problem directly imposed by the environment. The *socio-technic function* of an artifact involves its use in a social rather than a technological way. Our use of candles at formal dinner parties is a good example of socio-technic function. We certainly do not need candles to supply light in our modern, electrical world, but they do contribute to the social aspect of our lives at birthday parties, in investiture

in small things forgotten

ceremonies, and on Christmas trees. *Ideo-technic function* sees the use of artifacts in religious and ideological contexts. Votive candles in the Catholic Church, and the candles of the Jewish menora serve an ideo-technic function. Obviously, the same artifacts can function on all three levels much of the time. It is important that the archaeologist realize this and attempt to determine what kind of function his artifacts served for their owners and users.

The place of a household in the social scale had an important effect on the kinds of ceramics to be found in it. We know that the foodways of differing social classes differed significantly. Because of this, not only would families of modest means not be able to afford the more costly varieties of pottery, but the types would differ also as a result of differences in their use.

When we look at all the pottery representing the New England sites in question, it is immediately apparent that the entire collection divides into three, rather discrete groups. The first is characterized by a preponderance of plain, utility earthenwares, with very small quantities of delft, Rhenish stoneware, and slipware. This group is the smallest of the three, since it represents only those sites that predate the mid seventeenth century. The second group contains a broad variety of the fancier, imported wares that were scarce in the first, as well as a vast quantity of American-made utility wares. This group represents the period from the mid seventeenth century to the late eighteenth century. The third group, representing sites dating from about the time of the Revolution through the first quarter of the nineteenth century, is spectacularly different from the other two. Except for delftware, all of the fine imported ceramics of the second group are absent, replaced by the popular creamwares and pearlwares.

What is the significance of these groupings? They certainly reflect the known history of English and American ceramics in the two centuries between 1630 and 1830. But they also reflect three periods of Anglo-American cultural development. When we consider in greater detail the function and form of the pottery of these three periods, it gradually becomes clear that something more than simple technological change is involved.

The role of ceramics in the early decades of the American colonies reflects their function in the English culture that gave them birth. Since most of the first colonists were yeomen or husbandmen, the foodways of the English yeoman might provide us with an understanding of ceramic use in early Anglo-America. Jay Anderson's study of the foodways of the Stuart yeoman[4] shows that ceramics played a relatively minor role in food preparation and consumption. Cooking was usually done in metal vessels such as pots, kettles, and skillets. Food was served directly from the cooking pots, and eaten from trenchers—small wooden trays, usually with shallow depressions in their centers to hold liquid. Trenchers were communally used, with two or more "trencher mates" eating from a single one. Beverages were also drunk from common containers, which were of leather, pewter, pottery, or rarely glass. Communal food consumption from utensils of many materials other than pottery suggests that ceramics played an insignificant and minor role in the processing and eating of food.

There was an area in which ceramics played a more important role, that which related to the dairy. The English yeoman made extensive use of milk products. Cheese was a more important protein source than was meat, and the folk term for it was "white meat." The activities that centered on milk and cream storage and butter and cheese production involved ceramics in a central role. Early descriptions of dairy activities place great stress on cleanliness, and lead-glazed earthenware containers were preferred for ease of cleaning. Milk pans, colanders, jars, and crocks of earthenware might have been found in the yeoman's dairy. The importance of dairying was carried over into the New World. In 1627, the corporate livestock herds of the community of New Plimoth were divided among individual households. Only those animals that produced milk—cows and goats—were meticulously apportioned on a strict per-capita basis. Other animals, such as pigs, which were used for their meat, were not so carefully divided. Plymouth's role in cattle production in the 1630s might also reflect the importance of dairying. The cattle were traded to the new Massachusetts Bay Colony for other necessary commodities, and this trade was the mainstay of Plymouth's economy during that time.

The ceramics found in American sites of the first half of the seventeenth century are of the types and quantities such a pattern of ceramic use would indicate. The preponderance of plain utility wares from these sites, and their

Figure 3. Pipkin (a) and Frechen stoneware bottle (b)

forms—pans, jars, pitchers, colanders, and crocks—all suggest dairying activities. Little of the pottery from this period appears to be related to food preparation and consumption, and is limited to infrequent pipkins (see Figure 3a). These are small, three-legged cooking pots of a buff earthenware glazed in green or yellow, which were made both in England and the Low Countries. They are found in English postmedieval sites of the same period.

Marley Brown's study of probate inventories from

both Essex, England, and Plymouth, Massachusetts, dating to the first half of the seventeenth century also suggests dairying as the predominant activity with which ceramics were involved.[5] He found that ceramics were mentioned in only 15 percent of all inventories from Essex. These inventories were all taken room by room, and in those mentioning ceramics, 75 percent of the ceramics' were specifically located in the dairy. Economic status seems to have had no effect on this pattern, since no differences were seen in estates ranging in value from £18 to £800, with an estate exceeding £200 probably representing a well-to-do yeoman. In Plymouth, a similar picture emerges from the probate inventories. Although very few were taken on a room-by-room basis, roughly half of a sample of inventories from 1633 to 1660 clearly shows ceramics to be associated with dairying activities in the kitchen or hall. (The hall, in seventeenth-century terms, was the main downstairs room of a house and the center of a variety of activities.)

While Brown's study dealt specifically with inventories from a single colony, the results fit comfortably with archaeological collections from English colonial sites all along the eastern edge of North America. Thus, by combining archaeological and documentary information, we can draw a rather detailed picture of the use of ceramics in the time before 1660 in English America. Pottery was not common, and what was available was almost entirely imported from England. Although the local production of pottery had begun by the 1630s in both Virginia and New England, the market seems to have been local and the production limited, since so many imported utility wares have been found in sites of the period. The major use of pottery was in dairy production, and food was cooked in and eaten from utensils of other materials, metal and wood being the most common.

The dairying function of ceramics continues beyond 1660 and lasts well into the eighteenth century. The same basic set of pottery forms—milk pans, crocks, and jars—is found on site after site for over a century and a half. They are joined, as time goes on, by other types of pottery, and the second of our periods is set apart from the first by this diversity. Due in no small part to the quickening of commerce between England and the colonies following the Restoration, the appearance of the full inventory of English and German ceramics occurred at a rapid rate. But the way in which these new kinds of pottery were used seems somewhat different from that of contemporary England.

Such a difference makes sense when we remember that by this time the English colonies were occupied by people many of whom had never laid eyes on England. The first thing we notice in the archaeological collections is the relative scarcity of plates, and their very slow increase in numbers over time. In England, plates were commonly used by the late seventeenth century, and the delftware factories turned them out in sets. But in America, those few plates that have been found in archaeological sites seem to have served a different function, at least in part. It was common practice for the English yeoman to display pewter plates in an open court cupboard. Such a display clearly

in small things forgotten

indicates a socio-technic function for the pewter: to grace a family's parlor and to show one's neighbors that they are possessed of means. The plates that have come from sites of the second period in New England are mostly of delftware and are relatively large and elaborate, in contrast to the somewhat commonplace nature of most of the artifacts with which they are associated. They sometimes show wear on the bottom edge, resulting from being stood upright. One blue-and-white delftware plate, from Flowerdew Hundred, has two holes in the foot ring, intended to hold a string or wire for suspension much like modern souvenir plates. Ceramic cups and mugs, on the other hand, became very common after 1660, possibly suggesting that drinking vessels of pottery were being integrated into food-consumption patterns before plates were. Probate inventories show that wooden trenchers remained very common utensils until the late eighteenth century, so that we can suggest that the typical set of utensils for eating and drinking consisted of trencher and ceramic cup. Plates, on the other hand, might well have served the socio-technic function of public display.

We can guess that there might even have been some ideo-technic factors at work. Ivor Noël Hume has suggested that Puritan attitudes toward decoration of everyday objects might have had an effect on the delftware industry in the London area in the form of a reduction of the amount of decorated pottery before the Restoration.[6] We know that throughout the Middle Ages, the English were very sensitive to overelaboration in dress; one's social position was defined in part by how elaborately one was attired. The legislation that regulated such dress, the so-called sumptuary laws, had all been repealed by 1621 by decree of King James I. Yet in that same year, the governor of Virginia received orders to "Suppress drunkenness, gameing & excess in cloaths [and] not to permit any but ye Council & heads of hundreds to wear gold in their cloaths or to wear Silk . . ."[7] The Massachusetts Bay Colony legislated against ornate styles of personal dress in 1634. Such regulation of personal attire is of a socio-technic nature, but the attitudes that it reflected could well have held for other kinds of decorative elaboration. This would be particularly likely in a colony dominated by Puritan ideology. For example, an absence of decoration characterizes New England gravestones carved before 1670; while expertly carved, they are severely plain. This is in marked contrast to the ornate style of gravestone carving that had characterized English culture from a much earlier date. In its religious purity and cultural homogeneity, New England may show the effects of the Puritan philosophy on the decorative arts more clearly than old England, where the Puritans were but a part of the larger population, or in the other colonies, where they were even less numerous. If this is so (and it must remain only conjecture at this time), the use of gaily decorated plates for personal display may not have been looked upon with favor until late in the seventeenth century.

Another trend is indicated by the increase in cups, bowls, and mugs during the second period, a slow, steady

in small things forgotten

shift to individualized utensils. While trenchers, of perishable wood, cannot be counted archaeologically, the pottery drinking utensils can be, and they appear to increase in absolute numbers during this time.

The period from 1660 through 1760 was a time when pottery utensils were more fully incorporated into the foodways of Americans, and served a greater variety of functions, including at least one of a socio-technic nature. Brown's study of the probate inventories supports this conclusion in a general way. The socio-technic use of plates and other delftware pieces finds some support in a number of room-by-room inventories from the time. They show that such pieces were often located in the parlor. The parlor of a seventeenth-century house was its most formal room. It possessed almost a ceremonial significance, as the room where bodies were laid in state, honored guests received, and family treasures stored. Such a location for delft pieces in this room virtually guarantees their socio-technic function, since the room as a whole functioned similarly. The inventories also show a slow, steady increase in the number of plates, as well as increasing numbers of ceramic drinking vessels.

The dramatic change in ceramics that occurred after circa 1760 is certainly due in part to changes that took place in the English pottery industry. The perfection of creamware, in the 1760s, led to the first truly mass-produced pottery, more widely available at a lower cost than before. By this time, trade between England and the colonies was regular and intense. Although the colonial governments promoted various "Buy American" schemes, except for coarse utility wares and some slipwares English pottery still dominated the American domestic scene. Indeed, as the eighteenth century drew to a close, less and less domestic pottery was evident. The market had been cornered by the Staffordshire potteries, with which local potters could not compete.

The greater availability of English pottery is only a part of the picture, however. There appears to have been a change in the mode of ceramic use as well, related in some way to changing foodways, which preceded the initial availability of mass-produced wares. The contents of a single trash pit, excavated in the back yard of a downtown Plymouth, Massachusetts, house, illustrate this change dramatically. The pottery in this pit consisted of eight plates, eight chamber pots, and three bowls, in delftware; three mugs, a bowl, a teacup, a teapot lid, a saucer, and a plate, in English white salt-glazed stoneware; one agateware bowl; a slipware pitcher; four slip-decorated chamber pots; three crocks and five bowls of plain domestic earthenware; and one Whieldon-ware teapot. The pit dates to the 1760s and almost certainly represents the repository of a single family's refuse.

The most striking contrast between the contents of this pit and the pottery from earlier sites is in the preponderance of plates and chamber pots. Three domestic sites in the Plymouth area which dated to the late seventeenth and early eighteenth centuries, each occupied for nearly half a century, produced a total of only twenty-one plates. The trash pit seems to have been used for less than a decade, and its eight plates must represent but a fraction of the total number discarded by its users over a period of fifty years.

Chamber pots are similarly scarce in sites of the first two periods. Such pots are interesting artifacts which have been largely replaced in our modern world by indoor plumbing. They were an outlet for the expression of their makers' earthy humor on many occasions. Examples survive from the seventeenth century with faces modeled in three dimensions in their bottoms, and the king's initials were sometimes placed on their rims. Various mottoes exhorting their users to perform their bodily functions with dispatch were applied in slip on their sides. One of the more charming verses appears on certain pearlware chamber pots, lettered inside on the bottom:

Treat me nice and keep me clean
And I'll not tell what I have seen.

Sites that date later than 1760 show an identical pattern of ceramic types. Plates and chamber pots are found in great numbers, with the plates matching not only each other but saucers and cups as well. This seemingly sudden appearance of plates and chamber pots in significantly increased numbers calls for some explanation. A strong possibility is that this change reflects a new accommodation between individuals and their material culture. Gone now is the older, corporate emphasis, wherein sharing of technomic objects was the norm. In its place we see a one-to-one match, with people probably having their own individual plate and chamber pot. This would certainly be an expression of a newly emergent worldview characterized by order, control, and balance. A one person/one dish relationship is symmetrical, while a number of people sharing a single dish, or a single chamber pot, is definitely not. Balance and a greater importance of the individual characterize this new view of life. Again, the probate inventories support the archaeological conclusions and provide some additional insights. Trenchers continue to be listed through a part of the third period, but by the 1770s we note the presence of full sets of dishes, often more than one set per household. In the 1780s, complete services of porcelain, creamware, and stoneware appear in some inventories. The porcelain in these inventories is largely limited to tea sets, and probably demonstrates the adoption of the full-blown English tea ceremony for the first time. This custom can be considered as a good indicator of the re-Anglicization process that was at work at the time.

Porcelain is quite unusual in archaeological sites before 1800. It was not usually owned by families of modest estate, and its first appearance in the Plymouth inventories is in 1736, in the parlor of a merchant, accompanied by delft. The taking of tea in such a formal way is certainly a social event rather than a contribution to the survival, in a direct, technomic way, of the people drinking it, so that this association is expectable. Porcelain tea sets were probably socio-technic, a functional distribution supported by the location of this earliest occurrence. Socio-technic artifacts

in small things forgotten

may be much less liable to breakage than technomic artifacts, due to less frequent and more careful usage. A trash pit dating to circa 1835, in the same yard as the 1760 pit discussed earlier, contained a large amount of creamwares and pearlwares of the early nineteenth century but also porcelain teacups and saucers of the late eighteenth century. The best explanation of this early date for the porcelain was that it had been treated with greater care.

The two-hundred-odd years between the early nineteenth century and the early seventeenth reveal trends reflecting the changes in Anglo-American life we have suggested. Most obvious of these is the clear relationship between the early ceramic evidence and patterns of ceramic use as seen in the culture of the English yeoman and the appearance of highly individualized sets of dishes, cups, and chamber pots after 1760. The intermediate period shows the trends from the earlier, corporate mode of ceramic use to the later, individualized one. The inventories are quite supportive in most cases and contradictory in none. What is not too clear is any indication of regional variation during the second period, which we would expect to find in traditional folk cultures. But this is not surprising, since much of the pottery was imported and thus did not reflect regional variations in local manufacture.

There were, however, two traditions of locally produced pottery present in the colonies, one beginning as early as the 1620s and the other making its appearance in the last quarter of the seventeenth century. The first of these was the production of red-bodied, lead-glazed, and wheel-made utility wares, a continuation of an English tradition of coarse ware production which stretches back into the Middle Ages. In colonial America, increasing quantities of this utility ware were turned out by hundreds of potters, most of them serving a rather restricted market area. These wares do differ in a number of technical aspects, such as paste, glaze color, and minor variations in form, but are not as reflective of the kind of regional variation we might hope to find. The second tradition is that of the handmade, unglazed pottery which we call Colono ware, thought by many to have been produced by slaves for their own use. We shall see later how this pottery can inform us as to the nature of social interaction between African Americans and Anglo-Americans. But while neither of these ceramic traditions sheds light on regional variation between 1660 and 1760, a very different kind of artifact shows this in a highly detailed way. The tens of thousands of gravestones that stand in hundreds of cemeteries in New England are a remarkable source of such information, and it is to them that we now turn our attention.

4

remember me as you pass by

There is no better place to stand face-to-face with the past than in the old burying grounds of New England. They have not been significantly altered since the time of their use, and row on row of stones, with grim death's-heads and hopeful cherubs carved on them, look out on us just as they did on the people of the seventeenth and eighteenth centuries. From the designs of these stones, and the way they vary in time and space, we may learn much.

The mortuary art of colonial Anglo-America is unique in providing us with a tightly controlled body of material in which to observe stylistic change in material culture, and to relate this change to changes in the society that produced it. All archaeological data—artifacts, structures, sites—possess three inherent dimensions: space, time, and form. The organization of these data rests on describing them as accurately as possible in terms of these three dimensions. The location of an artifact within a building, of a building within its community, of a community in relation to other communities, alike and different, are all examples of the spatial dimension of archaeological data. We have already seen how important the dimension of time is. Proper and precise dating is the cornerstone of all studies of change over time. The formal dimension of archaeological data involves the physical aspects of artifacts, structures, and sites. "Delftware" is a formal category, denoting a type of pottery found on historic sites. Its cultural significance varies depending on differences in the other two dimensions. We have seen it serving either a technomic or a sociotechnic function, depending on where it is found (England or America) at the same time in the late seventeenth century, or in the same place at different times (America in the seventeenth and eighteenth centuries).

If we had at our disposal an extensive collection of artifacts that could be precisely controlled along each of these three dimensions, we would be able to consider variation along each dimension while holding the other two constant. Such control would allow the testing of various propositions relating to artifact change and culture change in a way rarely encountered in archaeological research. The gravestones of colonial New England provide us with just such a laboratory situation, since their spatial, temporal, and formal dimensions can be carefully calibrated and controlled.

Making use of the formal dimension of gravestone art involves understanding the designs carved on the stones in terms of their symbolism and determining their makers.

Again probate records prove valuable, for it is through their use that the carvers of the stones have frequently been identified. Entries in inventories of debts against the estate often specify payment for gravestones. While we cannot be certain that all such payments were made directly to the carver, when the stones of a number of deceased persons are seen to be the work of one man, and their inventories designate the men receiving payment, the carver's identity has been established. A few stones were signed, and account books and diaries of the carvers occasionally make specific reference to stones that can be seen today in some burying ground. All of this evidence combined permitted Harriette Forbes to identify 127 carvers in New England who were working before 1800. Her pioneering study remains to this day as one of the basic source books on the subject of New England gravestone art.[1]

Even when the maker cannot be identified from the documentary sources, it is usually possible to determine the town in which he was working. Most carvers distributed their product over a relatively small geographical area, perhaps thirty-odd miles across. Within such an area, distinctive styles of stones can be seen to concentrate in one town and become less common as we move away from it. In the case of a known carver, the central town is his residence, and the same applies to carvers who have not been named from the records. In most small New England communities, there simply was not enough business to keep a carver busy on a full-time basis, so we find that they pursued other trades as well. Since the vast majority of gravestone carvers working before 1800 were not full-time specialists, the way in which they learned and passed on designs was typical of traditional cultures. The combination of a small output of gravestones and a limited distribution of them produces a high level of spatial variation throughout the colonial period.

The identification of the carvers of the stones, their places of residence, and their periods of production provide us with a good control of the formal dimension of these artifacts. Their symbolism also can be determined to a great extent. Gravestones are a prime example of ideo-technic artifacts. A deep concern with death and the survival of the soul is central to all religions. Since we know a great deal about the changes in ideology in New England in the colonial era, the form of gravestones and their designs can be studied in terms of these changes.

Knowing the carvers of the stones and their places of residence also permits a high level of spatial control. The stones we see in graveyards today have been there since they were erected, although some have been moved within the precincts of the cemeteries by overzealous grounds keepers. For almost every stone, we can determine where it was made and where it ultimately was placed. In cemeteries that have not been rearranged, the relationship between the stones almost always reflects family groupings.

Since they are markers and memorials of the dead, gravestones carry the date of the individual's death. Probate data and other documentary sources show that most stones were erected a short time after the death of the individual, so that date of death and date of carving are close in time. This kind of temporal control enables us to isolate the occasional stone carved and erected sometime later, since each carver's work can be seen to develop and change through time.

By controlling the dimensions of time, space, and form so well, we can use gravestones to test and refine certain methods and assumptions that were developed initially in the context of prehistoric archaeology. One such method is the dating procedure known as *seriation*. Developed by the archaeologist James A. Ford,[2] this method rests on the fact that, over time, a graph of the popularity of any cultural trait will have a single peak. Styles of artifacts, dancing, vernacular speech, or music have small beginnings, grow in popularity until a peak is reached, and then fade away. If we were to chart the relative popularity of creamware in American historical sites by decades beginning in the 1760s, using a graph in which horizontal bars reflect its frequency by their width, a pattern shaped rather like a battleship viewed from above would result. Pearlware, which replaces creamware, would produce a similar pattern, but later in time. If we were ignorant of the actual date of the production of either creamware or pearlware, we could still place a series of sites that produced both relative to each other in time by arranging them in such a way that the frequency representations of creamware and pearlware each produced a smooth curve. If more pottery types were present, such a procedure would be even more precise and dependable. Suppose seven historic sites produced the following relative frequency of three pottery types: creamware, pearlware, and delftware.

Site	Delftware	Creamware	Pearlware
1	50%	40%	10%
2	90	10	0
3	0	0	100
4	0	40	60
5	10	60	30
6	0	20	80
7	70	30	0

There is only one possible order in which these seven sites can be arranged that places the three types in a sequence reflecting the gradual increase and decrease of each. This arrangement is only relative chronologically, and known dates of production of each type are necessary to fix the entire sequence in absolute time. Our relative ordering of the seven sites is:

Site	Delftware	Creamware	Pearlware
3	0%	0%	100%
6	0	20	80
4	0	40	60
5	10	60	30
1	50	40	10
7	70	30	0
2	90	10	0

in small things forgotten

The method of seriation was developed using pottery types from prehistoric sites in the lower Mississippi river valley. The assumption of the shape of the popularity curve of single types was a most reasonable one but remained an assumption in the process of developing the method. That such a pattern of change is exhibited by artifact popularity in time is demonstrated in cemetery after cemetery in New England, where the popularity trends of gravestone styles conform perfectly to the battleship-shaped graph under conditions of rigorous temporal and formal control. Not only do gravestones support the method's basic premise, but in certain instances we shall find exceptions and from these gain a further understanding of style change as it reflects behavior. The proportions of the battleship-shaped curves are also instructive. Long, slender battleships reflect slow change and traditional culture, while short, squat battleships are more typical of popular culture and rapid change.

Three basic designs were used by the stone carvers of New England between about 1680 and 1820.[3] The earliest of the three is a winged death's-head with blank eyes and a grinning visage. Earlier versions are quite ornate on occasion, but as time passed they became less elaborate. Sometime during the eighteenth century—the time varies according to location—the grim death's-heads were replaced by a new design, the winged cherub. Toward the end of the eighteenth century the cherubs were replaced in turn by the third basic design, a willow tree overhanging a pedestaled urn. In addition to these basic designs, there was a wide variety of other motifs used, but in one way or another most were derivative of the early, death's-head motif. Such variation was typical of rural areas, and much of this local variation was a function of relative isolation and the maintenance of traditional culture. In the urban centers of New England, however, death's-heads, cherubs, and urns were the carvers' main stock in trade. Graphing the three basic styles in a cemetery where they form the great majority of designs produces three nearly perfect battleship-shaped curves (see Figure 4).

This stylistic succession, repeated in cemetery after cemetery, is a clear index of important changes in the religious views of New Englanders. The period of decline of death's-heads coincides with the decline of orthodox Puritanism. In the late-seventeenth century, the Puritan Church was still dominant in the area. Likewise, death's-heads were the nearly universal style of gravestone decoration. The early part of the eighteenth century saw the beginnings of change in orthodoxy, culminating in the great religious revival movements of the mid eighteenth century known as the Great Awakening. Alan Ludwig[4] sees the Puritans as "iconophobic," feeling that to portray a cherub would be to introduce the image of a heavenly being, which could lead to idolatry. The death's-head was a more earthly and neutral symbol, serving as a graphic reminder of death and resurrection.

During the Great Awakening, in the period from the 1720s to the 1760s, revivalist preachers such as Jonathan Edwards preached a different approach to religion, in

1820-29

1810-19

1800-09

1790-99

1780-89

1770-79

1760-69

1750-59

1740-49

1730-39

1720-29

Figure 4. Succession of gravestone designs, Stoneham Cemetery, Massachusetts

which the individual was personally involved with the supernatural. Such a view was more compatible with designs such as the cherub; it also freed the iconography of the gravestone from the rigid adherence to one symbol, the death's-head, and the trend everywhere involved a softening of this harsh symbolism. Cherubs represent such a softening, but we shall encounter a variety of other truly wonderful designs that seem to have achieved the same effect.

It is at this point that the inscriptions on the stones become quite relevant. Each stone begins by describing the status of the deceased. "Here lies . . ." and "Here lies buried . . ." are typical early examples found with death's-heads on gravestones. Slowly these phrases were replaced by "Here lies buried the Body (. . . corruptible . . . what was mortal of) . . ." This slightly but significantly different statement reflects a tendency to emphasize that only a part of the deceased remains. The soul, the incorruptible or immortal portion, has gone to its eternal reward. Such descriptive phrases are more frequently seen on stones decorated with cherubs. The epitaphs that appear on many stones also add credence to this explanation of change in form over time. Early epitaphs, with death's-head designs, stress decay and life's brevity:

My youthful mates both small and great
Come here and you may see
An awful sight, which is a type
Of which you soon must be

Epitaphs with cherub stones, on the other hand, tend to stress resurrection, and later, heavenly reward:

Here cease thy tears, suppress thy fruitless mourn
his soul—the immortal part—has upward flown
On wings he soars his rapid way
to yon bright regions of eternal day

The final shift seen in gravestone design is to the urn-and-willow style. It is usually accompanied with a change in stone shape. While earlier stones have a round-shoul-dered outline, the later stones have square shoulders. "Here lies the body of . . ." is replaced by "In Memory of . . ." or "Sacred to the Memory of . . . ," statements that have very different meaning from those used earlier. The earlier stones are markers, designating the location of the de-ceased—at least in their mortal form. In contrast, "In Memory of . . ." is a memorial statement, and stones of this later type could be erected even if the body of the deceased was not beneath. Many of the later urn-and-wil-low-decorated stones are in fact cenotaphs, erected to com-memorate those buried elsewhere, as far distant as Africa, Batavia, and in one case—in the Kingston, Massachusetts, cemetery—"drowned at sea, lat. 39 degrees north, long. 70 degrees west." The urn-and-willow is not a graphic repre-sentation of either the mortal component or the immortal component of the individual but, rather, a symbol of com-memoration. This depersonalization is reflected in the more common theme of epitaphs found with the design. While the earlier themes still occurred, they were joined by another, one that simply lauded the individual in terms of his worldly achievements. These changes seem to indicate a secularization of the religion.

The sequence of styles described occurred in England as well. There the cherub design was quite commonly used by the beginning of the Georgian period, in 1715, and urns appear on stones as early as 1760. The colonial world followed the English pattern, but in certain areas lagged it by approximately half a century. This difference was an important factor in the initial appearance of the cherub style in America and its subsequent diffusion across the countryside.

This simple sequence of three basic designs over a period of a century is very indicative of religious change in Anglo-America. But its delineation is but a beginning of the ways in which mortuary art can inform us about colonial America. Let us consider these design changes in time and space in greater detail. In Massachusetts, three different patterns of stylistic evolution are apparent. Each represents the accommodation by mortuary art of the changes in ideology that were taking place, but this accommodation was quite different depending upon where it took place. In the urban center of Boston one development occurs, in the adjacent countryside another, and in the deep countryside yet a third.

Boston in the late seventeenth century had become the cosmopolitan center of Massachusetts Bay Colony. Cambridge, across the Charles River, boasted a growing college in Harvard, which was established in 1636. The population was sufficiently large to require the services of a number of gravestone carvers. The Lamson family of Charlestown, who produced stones through most of the eighteenth century, seem to have been full-time workers at the trade, in sharp contrast to their rural counterparts. Lamson stones are commonplace throughout New England, and were exported at least as far as Charleston, South Carolina. This family, whose gravestone production covered three generations, were important style setters; many rural stone carvers attempted to copy their work, with varying degrees of success.

The cherub design made an early appearance in both Boston and Cambridge, and stones bearing angels on their tops were carved and erected from the first years of the eighteenth century. However, the numbers of cherubs adorning gravestones in Cambridge and in Boston differed greatly. Cambridge, as represented by the cemetery situated today in Harvard Square, saw cherubs gain in popularity at a slow but steady rate from the first decade of the eighteenth century until they reached a majority in the last decade. In Boston, on the other hand, cherubs were never common, though always present during the 1700s.

Remembering that the cherub design appeared late in the seventeenth century in England, it is reasonable to explain the popularity of this design in Cambridge as the result of the Harvard intellectual and ecclesiastical community. This explanation receives strong support from the gravestones themselves. Sixty-five percent of all cherub stones in the Cambridge burying ground mark the resting places of high-status individuals, precisely those people who would have been most *au courant* with the latest style in the home country. Stones, inscribed in Latin, marking the burial locations of college graduates—military leaders, church officials, a president of Harvard, and Harvard teachers—all have cherubs carved upon them. In contrast, only 5 percent of all death's-head stones in this cemetery mark such high-status persons.

Within the community of Cambridge, then, we might suggest two groups, one the more progressive elite, who preferred the cherub design, and the other the more traditional group of lower status, whose religious views were more consistent with the symbolism represented by the grim death's-heads. Across the Charles River the same pattern appears, but in the absence of as large a group of academicians and church leaders the number of cherub-decorated stones to be seen is predictably smaller. The retention of the death's-head design in Boston is quite long-lived. The cemeteries of downtown Boston are the only ones that contain square-shouldered stones inscribed "In Memory of . . ." dating to the 1830s and decorated with simple death's-heads. By this late date, we might suggest, the design had lost much of its original symbolic value but does reflect a strongly traditional component of the urban population.

Since the carvers of this urban center were producing both death's-heads and cherubs throughout the eighteenth century, those changes in religious views that occurred should be accommodated iconographically simply by a change in the proportions of each type carved. There was

in small things forgotten

no need to modify either design, and we see that early and late cherubs or death's-heads differ little, save for a slow trend toward less elaborate decorative embellishment. The urban pattern differs from the rural patterns of design change in just this respect.

In those areas that lay beyond the city of Boston but were situated close enough to be directly affected by the urban culture, a very different stylistic sequence occurred. The cherub design first was introduced into the urban society. From there, the preference for its use spread slowly across the countryside. Since gravestone art is so rigorously controlled in its spatial and temporal aspects, it has been possible to measure the rate of this spread. It was remarkably constant, proceeding at roughly one mile per year.[5]

Scituate, Massachusetts, is a small town some twenty-five miles southeast of Boston. A coastal community, it was founded in 1634. The work of two of its eighteenth-century gravestone carvers, Jacob Vinal and his son, Jacob Vinal, Jr., shows a direct evolution from death's-heads to cherubs (see Figure 5). The earlier stones are naïve copies of Lamson death's-heads; the source is obvious, extending to the use of figs in pairs on footstones, a Lamson specialty. There is little ambiguity in these first death's-heads. Although crudely carved, they are unmistakably skulls. In time, however, the design was softened by means of emphasizing the nose details over the teeth. Stones from the 1730s, while still blank-eyed, have noses that look more like smiling mouths, and the teeth have been dropped to a less prominent position. Jacob Vinal died in 1736, and his son continued to

Figure 5. Development of gravestone design by Jacob Vinal and his son Jacob Vinal, Jr., of Scituate, Massachusetts

in small things forgotten

develop and elaborate the design. By the 1740s pupils had been added to the blank eyes, further animating the face. These first pupils seem to have been inspired by the hole made by the compasses used to draw the orbits, which had become round rather than oval like the ones typical of death's-heads. The addition of pupils, which became more elaborate through the 1740s, created a face in which the teeth, now almost vestigial, no longer were seen as teeth, since Vinal frequently carved three rows of them. By the end of the forties, the common gravestone used in Scituate was neither death's-head nor cherub, but, rather, a distinctive folk design in its own right. But it was still possessed of wings, so that when the first cherub stones were carved by Vinal, the change was simple and involved only a change of faces.

This sequence demonstrates the response of rural carvers not too distant from Boston to the changes in ideology that were sweeping New England at the time. The evolution exactly matches the period of the Great Awakening, and its essential quality is the softening of the grim death's-head symbol in a situation in which the cherub design had not yet gained acceptance. It is a graphic compromise, one that seems to have satisfied the people of the area, judging from its universality. This compromise may have been achieved through a process which Peter Benes has called "visual punning," the creation of symbols which carry a double meaning.[6] The heart, a life symbol, was often incorporated in subtle ways into an otherwise grim symbol of death, the winged skull (see Figure 6). At times

Figure 6. *Visual punning by Jacob Vinal, Scituate, Massachusetts*

the wings join over the head to form a heart-shaped space between them. Hearts were used in the location where a mouth would normally be found by both the Vinals and stone carvers farther south in the Plymouth area (see Nathaniel Fuller, Figure 7). Certainly Jacob Vinal Jr.'s fully developed spirit faces were potentially powerful visual puns. One could choose to see them as symbolizing death if the atrophied teeth were perceived as a part of a death's-head, or one could instead see these teeth as something entirely different while considering the elaborated nose as a mouth. To what extent such punning symbolism was consciously employed by the carvers we will never know. What is important is that these faces were particularly appropriate for parishes which had been split by the Great Awakening into progressive and conservative factions, as we know many of the churches in the Scituate area to have been. Further support for such a proposition is provided by Peter Benes' study of two other carvers in the Scituate area, known only as the North River Carvers. Their work is

in small things forgotten

remarkably similar to that of the Vinals in its technical execution; all four men used a distinctive chip carving style to render various decorative elements. But the North River Carvers, after only a brief flirtation with heart-shaped elements, retained a conservative death's-head design, while the Vinals were animating the faces on their stones. The parishes where stones by the North River Carvers are to be found were those of wealthy shipbuilders, whose religious views remained conservative, unaffected by the Great Awakening through a refusal to associate with unorthodox church members, and by banning not only itinerant preachers, but also organs and hymnals from their churches. At the same time, their neighbors, farmers and fishermen of more modest means, embraced the break from the old orthodoxy, and this division is clearly visible in the iconography of the stones that stand today in the parish churchyards.

The Scituate development is not unique; it is repeated again and again in towns removed from Boston at about the same distance. A remarkable similar evolution takes place in the area of Wrentham, south and west of Boston. In Groton, Massachusetts, thirty miles northwest of Boston, the carver William Park developed an identical sequence. In his case, however, the development was more rapid, since he did not arrive in New England until 1745. His earliest stones are death's-heads, including some skillful copies of Lamson stones, but in the short span of a decade he had evolved the death's-head into a cherub.

In all of these cases, acceptance of cherubs took place

before the carvers had an opportunity to develop their designs too far beyond the prototypical death's-head. Still present were wings and a face area that could be transformed to a true cherub face with a minimum of change. Deeper in the countryside, the preference for cherubs did not arrive until later, by which time the carvers had evolved the death's-head into a completely new series of designs.

In cemetery after cemetery in the Plymouth, Massachusetts, area, we encounter strange faces atop the stones. Mouthless, blank-eyed faces with swirling hair, death's-heads with heart-shaped mouths, and light-bulb-shaped bald heads with T-shaped mouths, resemble nothing we might see in Boston, Cambridge, Scituate, or Groton. These Plymouth designs dramatically reflect the effect of isolation and traditional culture on gravestone design. However strange and exotic they seem at first, they were nonetheless derivative from the earlier, death's-head design.

The sequence of stylistic evolution in the Plymouth County area of Massachusetts is one of the most complex in all of New England (see Figure 7). In its unfolding, we witness a radiation of styles, the work of carvers in neighboring towns in the area. It has its beginnings, as do the other sequences we have examined, in a basic death's-head design. The stone carver who began the evolution away from this first motif was Nathaniel Fuller of Plympton, Massachusetts, grandson of Samuel Fuller, *Mayflower* passenger and an original settler of Plymouth.[7] Fuller's early death's-heads already show differences from those else-

in small things forgotten

William Cushman   Ebenezer Soule   Nathan Hayward

Nathaniel Fuller

Figure 7. The Plymouth sequence

where in New England. His trademark was a mouth element shaped like a heart. Fuller seems to have placed teeth in his death's-heads only occasionally. More typical was the heart mouth standing alone. The wings are in evidence, but very early in his career he consistently reversed the direction of the curve marking the ends of the feathers on alternate rows. The result was a heart-mouthed death's-head surrounded by radiating undulating lines. The face still retains the death's-head's blank, oval eyes, but already the design had moved away from the full-blown winged skull. Fuller's version of the death's-head is found throughout the Plymouth County area in the 1740s. In turn, it formed the inspiration for at least three subsequent developments.[8]

From the late 1740s until the 1760s, Ebenezer Soule of Plympton, William Cushman of Middleborough, and Nathan Hayward of Bridgewater all carved stones inspired by Fuller's stylized death's-heads. The three towns are close neighbors, fitting within a circle only ten miles in diameter. These three derived motifs share in one common feature; the transformation or removal of the wings that characterized Fuller's designs. Cushman's stones are adorned by faces with T-shaped mouths, derived from the Fuller heart mouths, and the wings are either changed to arcs behind the head, with feathers still indicated, or to simple arcs showing no feather ends but occasionally having complex scroll devices between them.

Hayward developed the design in a somewhat different fashion. He made the wings of Fuller's death's-heads curl up into a tight hairdo, an effect foreshadowed by the undulating lines formed by the ends of feathers on Fuller's designs. In most cases, new wings were added to these faces, which are further enlivened by a mouth reminiscent of a bird's beak. This mouth was almost always developed from the line at the base of the face formed by the compasses that drew the circle that outlined it.

in small things forgotten

Fuller's Plympton neighbor Ebenezer Soule also transformed Fuller's undulating lines into hair, but unlike Nathan Hayward, he developed a "Medusa" type of head for his gravestones. The earlier ones exhibit short hair, waving moderately to the top of the decorative field, but as time went on, Soule elaborated the hair style into one that alternated waves with tight curls. In further contrast with Hayward's faces, Soule's were never given wings, and most have no mouths at all.

We can see that all three men developed the earlier modified death's-heads into designs that resembled neither death's-head nor cherub. Fuller died in 1750, but it is almost certain that, had he lived, he, too, would have transformed his death's-head further from its original form. One of his last stones, carved in 1748, shows no wings, but scrolls, which resemble in a general way Soule's wavy locks or Hayward's tightly curled hairdos.

The people of rural Plymouth County developed a preference for the cherub design at the beginning of the 1760s. By this time, there was no simple way for the local carvers to develop their designs into a cherub motif, and the gravestones of this period show that they simply abandoned the older folk symbols and began carving cherubs on their stones. Of the three, Hayward, in attaching wings to his strange faces, made the least change, extensive though it was. Soule's Medusas, and Cushman's blank-eyed, T-mouthed faces shared nothing with the cherubs, which were becoming popular. All three men made the change rather rapidly, and by the end of the decade of the sixties, all of Plymouth County gravestone art was characterized by cherub designs quite similar one to another.

Soule left Plympton in 1769 and moved to Hinsdale, New Hampshire, where he continued carving through the 1780s. Granite stones in the area around Hinsdale are decorated by both the Medusa design and the newer cherub. Soule produced both the earlier and later designs throughout this later part of his career, which might indicate that the people in the Hinsdale area had not been quite as ready to adopt the cherub design, being somewhat further removed from the Boston center than was Plympton.

A further complication is seen in a simplified version of the Medusa design which was used in both Plympton and Hinsdale to mark the graves of children. These children's stones continued to be produced in the Plymouth County area well into the 1770s. We see the retention of an outmoded design in a specialized context. The retention of an older style for children's graves has been observed elsewhere in New England, where a slightly higher percentage of children than adults have graves marked by death's-heads at any given time. This pattern may well show generational differences in design preferences, since the gravestones of adults were probably more often selected by their children, while children's stones were obviously selected by adults.

That something more might have been involved is suggested by the stones marking the graves of two adults in Princeton, Massachusetts. Both have a variant of the simpli-

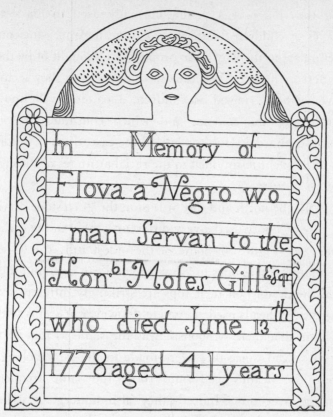

In Memory of Flova a Negro wo man Servan to the Hon.ᵇˡ Mofes Gill Eſqr who died June 13ᵗʰ 1778 aged 41 years

Figure 8. Gravestone of Flova, Princeton, Massachusetts

fied Medusa design, but in this case the stones mark the resting place of two adults who were not members of the free society in which they had lived. They are described in the inscriptions as "Flova, a negro womanservant" (1778) (see Figure 8) and "Thomas, a Negro manservant" (1783) "to the honorable Moses Gill." It is very likely that Flova was a slave; Thomas may not have been since Massachusetts manumitted its slaves in the same year that he died.

But the choice of a design normally used to mark the graves of children for these two African Americans could well relate to the way these people were thought of by their owners or masters. Whether slave or servant, they seemed to have been viewed as children, a pattern well known throughout the colonies and which continues in some places to this day. If this is indeed the case, these two stones stand as silent testimonial to the racial attitudes of the eighteenth century.

To the north and east of Boston the gravestone carvers of Essex County used a very different symbol in the earliest years (see Figure 9). Some of the oldest fully carved and decorated gravestones in New England can be found there, and the designs on their tops are strikingly different from the death's-heads used elsewhere. However, it seems safe to assume that their symbolism was the same as that of the death's-head, since they were made in the same colony as were the death's-heads and show the same frequency change over time. Indeed, they also undergo a stylistic evolution in the eighteenth century identical to that shown by winged skulls elsewhere. Their earliest form is that of an oval face with somewhat squared mouth and nose and a pair of birds meeting beak to beak over the forehead. The detail of these birds became simplified in time, and by the 1730s, six-pointed stars enclosed in circles were flanking the face, squeezing the birds aside. The birds vanished by the end of that decade, and until the 1750s, faces and stars were the standard motif. During this time, the face became the most schematic and rectilinear in delineation. It was

Harvard, Massachusetts

Connecticut   Essex County

Figure 9. The sequence in Essex County, Massachusetts, and its derivatives in Connecticut and in Harvard, Massachusetts

enclosed with a double outline, indications of which can be seen in earlier versions of the motif. During the 1750s, wings were added to the face, and the result was a cherub, although yet somewhat schematic in the rendering of the features. This rectilinear face was softened in time after the addition of the wings, and by the 1770s the standard design of the Essex County carvers was a reasonable cherub. This development is quite similar to that seen in Scituate, Groton, Wrentham, and other communities that were rural but in proximity to Boston.

An evolution similar to that which occurred in the Plymouth area also takes place within this tradition. Jonathan Worcester, a gravestone carver in Harvard, Massachusetts—roughly as far from Boston as is Plympton—adopted the Essex County design during its most schematic phase, in the 1740s. Its use by Worcester in the more distant town of Harvard was different from that seen in subsequent years in the Essex County area. Worcester "froze" the design, changing it not at all throughout the time he placed it atop his stones. At his death in 1754, his son Moses took up the design, altering it only slightly. In the early 1760s, with the popularity of the cherub design reaching Harvard, Moses Worcester was unable to develop the motif directly into a cherub. He abandoned it completely, and his new cherubs were thoroughly conventional and shared with the earlier design only a distinctive style of lettering and identical side elements on the stone.

Yet a third development from the original Essex County style took place, and it shows us again how the dominant stylistic tradition can work to bring about rapid change. William Park evolved his death's-heads into cherubs in only ten years in Groton, Massachusetts, after his arrival from Scotland. Joshua Hempstead of New London, Connecticut, is known from his diary to have been carving gravestones in the Essex County style in the second decade of the eighteenth century. Hempstead's connections with this tradition are both complex and less clear than one

in small things forgotten

might hope. He may in fact have only been inscribing stones sent to him fully carved by John Hartshorn, one of the early carvers of Essex County, and Hempstead's brother-in-law. Hartshorn himself removed to Norwich, Connecticut, in 1719, and presumably continued his craft in his new surroundings. But whether the early faces and birds of southeastern Connecticut were the work of either or both men is of less significance than the development that this design undergoes in its new environment. Here we see a rapid direct transformation into a full cherub form. The change takes only a decade to be complete. Once again we can see the rate of change being a function of the prevailing tastes and styles they generate from place to place. Slow change, with local diversification and elaboration, is the rule in remote rural areas. Where the locale is near a center of rapidly changing style, with a more popular than traditional form of culture, changes are more rapid. This difference probably accounts for the temporal priority of cherubs in both Rhode Island and Connecticut. Both Connecticut and Rhode Island carvers changed over to cherub designs before those in Massachusetts. The sequence in these two colonies more closely follows the English one in the time of stylistic succession.

Tiny Rhode Island in the early eighteenth century had as its commercial and intellectual focus the port city of Newport. Newport was the home of a number of gravestone carvers in the eighteenth century, and from the beginning their work is quite sophisticated and reflective of English styles. The preponderance of gravestones in Rhode

Island that date to the eighteenth century are the product of various Newport carvers. The result is an early appearance of cherubs, with a corresponding eclipsing of the death's-head design. Rhode Island was also a colony noted for religious tolerance, and its primary religion was Baptist. The strong Puritan influence on gravestone iconography was missing as a result, so the combined cosmopolitan nature of the population of Newport and a more receptive religious atmosphere was more than ample reason for the rapid rise of the cherub design in the colony.

Such was not the case in Connecticut, which, like Massachusetts Bay, was a Puritan colony. The stylistic sequence there seems more to follow the urban Boston-Cambridge pattern, with one major difference. The Connecticut river valley, which ran south through the center of the colony, was probably New England's most fertile region. In contrast to the subsistence farmer of rural Massachusetts Bay Colony, the farmers of the Connecticut Valley, and to a lesser extent of the Thames, to the east, were merchant farmers. Tobacco was an important cash crop until the second half of the eighteenth century, and much of the population of the rich river valley could afford to be aware of the latest styles in the home country. The gravestone art of Connecticut can be seen to develop in these rich valleys and spill over into the adjacent countryside. The elaborate red-sandstone grave markers of the Connecticut Valley are closer in over-all style to their English counterparts than any in New England. Yet they bear the mark of traditional

in small things forgotten

culture as well in a certain naïveté and in the somewhat simpler angel faces that adorn them.

Under special circumstances, differing rates of stylistic evolution can create a misleading pattern. If we chart the pattern of death's-head popularity in cemeteries on the outer reaches of Cape Cod, a curve is produced that is inconsistent with the basic assumption of archaeological seriation. Rather than having a single popularity peak early in the eighteenth century, the death's-head on Cape Cod faded in popularity until the 1750s and then became popular again, not returning to its mid-century low point until almost 1800.

A close examination of the known sources of the stones decorated with winged skulls tells what happened to produce such a "wasp-waisted" curve. Until mid-century, Cape Cod was basically agrarian and participated in a land-based market exchange with Plymouth—not surprising in view of the fact that the Cape was originally a part of Plymouth Colony. The soils of the Cape were thin and became exhausted in the middle of the eighteenth century. Town after town turned to fishing as a new economic pursuit, and the time of the establishment of the first fishing fleets in the outer Cape towns coincides with the beginning of the second period of death's-head popularity. Cape Cod is a vast sand bar, with little stone of the kind needed for gravestones. As a result, there were no gravestone carvers living on the Cape. Stones in the cemeteries of Cape Cod were all made by carvers living elsewhere.

Earlier, almost all Cape gravestones were imported from Plymouth, and we may see the work of Nathaniel Fuller and Ebenezer Soule in almost every cemetery on the Cape. When the Cape towns turned to fishing, they began to obtain their stones from Boston. The shift to Boston as a prime source of gravestones resulted in the renewed popularity of death's-heads, since they remained the most common type produced there until the end of the eighteenth century.

In a case such as this, the importance of the controls available to the student of mortuary art becomes obvious. If it were not possible to identify the sources of the stones with such precision, we would be left to wonder what had caused the peculiar pattern of death's-head popularity. Prehistoric archaeology rarely enjoys such a control over its data, and the lesson to be learned from this example is that irregularities in the data of prehistory, which might seem to be the result of improper chronological ordering, may in fact result from shifting patterns of exchange and distribution of various commodities. Such changes would be expected to occur along boundaries between various sociopolitical units, while in their centers a more regular and expectable rate and mode of change and succession might be seen.

This assumption is borne out by other gravestone data. A pattern not unlike that of Cape Cod occurred along the boundary between Rhode Island and Massachusetts Bay in the mid eighteenth century. Stylistic curves for cherub and death's-head are the most irregular along this line. The irregularity is the result of slight shifts in gravestone trading patterns, with Rhode Island cherubs alternating with Massachusetts Bay death's-heads in a somewhat random pattern. Cemeteries ten or more miles distant from the boundary, on the other hand, produce regular, ordered progressions of the two styles.

The stylistic trends of gravestone art also lend further support to the pattern of Anglo-American culture change outlined in Chapter 2. Unfortunately, there are only a very few stones that date to the period before 1660. The earliest stone in New England, situated in Ipswich, Massachusetts, is crudely lettered with the initials E.L. and dates to 1642. By the 1660s we see a few stones, competently lettered but undecorated. Death's-heads begin to appear regularly by the 1680s, as do the elaborate bird-flanked faces of Essex County. Why there are no gravestones from the earliest years of the colonies is not clear, although it has been suggested that they may have mostly been made from wood and thus have long since vanished. Grave markers of wood were common in parts of England at the time, and inventories make occasional mention of "Grave rails," as such wooden markers were called. In form, the grave rail resembled the headboard of a bedstead and was set in the ground parallel to the body of the deceased, with a post at the head and foot and the board between. In any case, the earliest decorated stones certainly reflect English usage, although the date of change to peculiarly American styles is somewhat later than our model would suggest.

However, religious institutions and their artifacts are

known to be the most conservative aspects of a culture, resisting change. The use of Gothic architecture for churches in our own society, the retention of the earlier pit house by the Hopi for a ceremonial chamber long after the development of masonry dwellings, and the Mandan Indians' retention of their old long house for a medicine lodge after their dwellings had changed from rectangular to circular are good examples of this kind of religious conservatism.

By the beginning of the eighteenth century, roughly halfway through our second period, we can see clearly the result of isolation in the rural sector of the colonial world. The Medusas of Plymouth, the masklike faces of Jonathan Worcester, and Vinal's animated carvings have no counterpart in England. Not only are these local styles radically different from contemporary English designs but also from each other. The period before circa 1760 is characterized by the greatest degree of regional variation in gravestone design. Carvers working only twenty miles apart were evolving very different motifs. This half century of great regional variation has all the hallmarks of traditional culture. Yet, in the cities, whether Boston, New Haven, or Newport, English styles were closely followed, and it is from these centers that the new designs' popularity spread over the countryside. By the beginning of the third period, the cherub design reigned almost absolute. The process of re-Anglicization can be seen in every cemetery in New England. The cherub is not only a popular English design of

in small things forgotten

the time; it is as typical of the Renaissance as the sober death's-head is of the medieval period which came before.

The new emphasis on the individual that is found in the third period can be seen to have an effect even after death. As we have seen, urn-and-willow-decorated stones are often simply memorials to individuals, even when the body of the deceased is not present in the burying ground. Such careful attention given to accounting for a person through a memorial is new at this time, nothing corresponding to it occurring earlier. Indeed, it is not unusual to find single stones, from earlier in the eighteenth century, that mark the resting places of husband and wife as well as children. Group interment of this type is typical of the earlier periods, and the contemporary concept of the churchyard was consistent with such a practice. Registers of churchyards invariably list far more interments than there are stones to account for them. Not everyone received a gravestone in the earlier periods, but unless we are able to conduct excavations in these cemeteries, the exact relationship between the numbers and groupings of the deceased and the markers in the cemetery will remain unknown. What is known is that the seventeenth- and eighteenth-century concept of a burying ground was that of a finite space that would hold all the deceased members of a parish regardless of how congested the space became. Diarists of the period mention bits of bone and teeth seen in the earth excavated for a new grave. Hamlet's remembrance of Yorick came about through just such circumstances, and

Shakespeare was almost certainly drawing from his knowledge of grave digging in Elizabethan England.

The literal packing of a small plot of consecrated ground was typical of colonial burial practices, but toward the end of the eighteenth century, New Englanders began the practice of burial in small family plots. Such tiny cemeteries are scattered throughout rural Massachusetts and almost always date to the last decade of the eighteenth century or later. By the early nineteenth century, the concept of the modern cemetery had appeared, with carefully designated lots and only one body per grave pit.

We see, then, that at just the time when New Englanders were beginning to use ceramics in the English fashion, with a new emphasis on individual matched services, they were also revising the manner in which they disposed of their dead. In two diverse practices, the change was very similar and might well reflect a wholly new way of looking at the world in which they lived.

i would have the howse
stronge in timber

With dates painted on their chimneys, their lawns neatly mowed, and room after room of period furniture, the historic houses of America proclaim their presence. Few towns or cities are without some kind of historic house museum, and indeed, places like Colonial Williamsburg in Virginia and Old Sturbridge Village in Massachusetts form extensive collections of such buildings. Such importance vested in old houses is not misplaced. The house is our most important buffer against the elements. Shelter is basic to human existence, and the earliest known forms are over one million years old. At Olduvai Gorge, in Tanzania, the archaeologist Louis Leakey excavated a simple ring of stones thought to represent a rudimentary foundation of a shelter built by our earliest ancestors, the australopithecine man-apes of southern and eastern Africa. Whether a crude brush-and-bough affair built by the nomadic Siriono Indians of Bolivia for a single night's use, or an elegant mansion on the beach at Newport, Rhode Island, the house forms the focus of that basic social unit of the human species, the family. People are conceived, are born, and die in houses; in preindustrial cultures, the house is at the same time the domestic center and the location of most production of essential artifacts. The form of a house can be a strong reflection of the needs and minds of those who built it; in addition, it shapes and directs their behavior. Small wonder that so much of archaeology concerns itself with the excavation and interpretation of domestic structures of almost endless variety.

The distinction between *vernacular* and *academic* building traditions is a critical one, since each reflects different aspects of the culture that created the buildings. Vernacular building is folk building, done without benefit of formal plans. Such structures are frequently built by their occupants or, if not, by someone who is well within the occupants' immediate community. Vernacular structures are the immediate product of their users and form a sensitive indicator of these persons' inner feelings, their ideas of what is or is not suitable to them. Consequently, changes in attitudes, values, and worldview are very likely to be reflected in changes in vernacular architectural forms. Academic architecture proceeds from plans created by architects trained in the trade and reflects contemporary styles of design that relate to formal architectural orders. It is much less indicative of the attitudes and lifestyles of the occupants of the buildings it creates. Vernacular building is an aspect of traditional culture, and academic architecture of popular

　　　　　　　in small things forgotten

culture. The change in Anglo-American building from the early seventeenth century to the end of the eighteenth century is essentially a picture of the slow development of vernacular forms under an increasing influence of the academic styles that were their contemporaries.

The evidence that permits us to understand the development of domestic architecture in Anglo-America is of three types. The first comprises all of the surviving structures from the period, both in England and America. The second consists of excavated remains and as such is limited only to those portions of a building that survived belowground. Finally, certain documentary materials are useful, including land titles and deeds, probate materials, and building contracts. Surviving buildings are subject to certain limitations, which we have already briefly considered. There is no guarantee that they are surely representative of their times. The factors that allow the survival of one house and the destruction of another are probably numerous and complex, but it seems a reasonable assumption that the simpler and ruder houses of early America have long since vanished. On certain occasions, modest houses have been built onto in different directions, so that careful analysis of the various "builds" exhibited by a house can isolate the original core structure. Too, it was not unusual for a house to be dismantled in order to obtain materials for the construction of a newer one. The subterranean remains of a house, which are observed through excavation, have survived the passage of time in a far less selective way than have whole structures. It is extremely unlikely that any building constructed in the past has vanished without a trace. These traces are often underground, however, and must be exposed with a shovel and trowel to be studied and understood. Even when this is accomplished, two other aspects of them must be considered: *focus* and *visibility*. *Focus* means the degree to which a pattern of postholes, cellars, and hearths can be "read" clearly as to how it represents the structure that once stood over it. *Visibility* means the actual amount of physical remains, however clearly or ambiguously they might be perceived. Sites can have poor focus and high visibility, or any combination of the two. For example, a house that had continuous stone footings as a foundation, a cellar, and substantial hearth, and which was not remodeled later, would provide an archaeological pattern of high focus and visibility. The tavern on Great Island in Wellfleet was such a site, and its architecture could be understood in some detail. On the other hand, the archaeological evidence of earthfast buildings usually has good focus, but very low visibility. In most instances, all that remains to be seen are the holes in which the posts were set, large rectangular stains marking the limits of the holes, and darker stains within, marking the location of the posts themselves. On occasion, one also finds the bases of hearths and/or small subfloor cellars. The stains marking the location of the posts are very faint, and usually can be seen clearly only when damp, either just after they have been exposed, or sprayed with a fine mist of water. But they do show in their pattern of arrangement the size and orientation of the house which once stood over them.

in small things forgotten

Even if the visibility of a house site is high, the focus can be low if there has been extensive alteration, remodeling, and change over a long period of time. A longer duration of occupation tends to reduce the focus of a house's underground remains while increasing the visibility. Houses that have burned in place have a higher visibility and focus than those that were either moved to another site or dismantled in place. House construction that intrudes well below grade also increases both the focus and visibility of the remains. The ideal feature for architectural study would be the remains of a house that was built with wall trenches, deep chimney base, and cellars, was occupied for a relatively brief period of time, was not added onto in any way, and burned in place. One such foundation was excavated at Flowerdew Hundred. It was the remains of a house built sometime during the third quarter of the eighteenth century which had burned during the first twenty years of the nineteenth. The house was a one-room structure, with a full brick cellar, entered through an exterior bulkhead, and a chimney at the opposite end. There was no evidence of rebuilding or adding rooms, so that what was excavated was the remains of the house as it had been when first constructed. The heat of the fire must have been intense, for it turned the subsoil red to a depth of two feet. Hundreds of mud wasp nests, which had been under the eaves, were fired to the hardness of pottery. No attempt appears to have been made to recover nails and other structural hardware from the ashes, and thousands of nails as well as hinges and latches were recovered, in remarkably rust-free condition, having been made so by the heat of the fire. Sites such as these are quite rare, however, and our understanding of the various forms of early American building comes from less explicit archaeological evidence combined with the many buildings that have fortunately survived the passage of three centuries' time.

If the story we have so far gleaned from pottery fragments and grave markers is a true indication of the way we have changed since the seventeenth century in our way of organizing and looking out upon our world, then a similar pattern of change is to be sought in changing building styles. Houses of the earliest period in Anglo-America should both resemble their English prototypes most closely and in some way provide evidence of a corporate lifestyle and a very organic integration. In time these should diverge and localize in form until they come under the impact of the academic traditions of the later eighteenth century.

If we were to rely only on the evidence of standing buildings, an oversimplified view of America's earliest architectural diversity would almost certainly result. The surviving evidence aboveground is remarkably homogeneous in form. While there are notable exceptions, the antique buildings of New England are predominantly of one form, the classic "salt box" house with a central chimney and rear kitchen projection (see Figure 10a), and in the Chesapeake, end chimney houses of one-room depth predominate (see Figure 10b). It would seem reasonable to assume that similar house forms existed in the earlier seventeenth century as standard types. But when the evidence from both archaeol-

Figure 10a. New England salt-box house

ogy and documentary sources is taken into account, a very different picture emerges, one of considerable diversity, owing in large part to the corresponding demographic diversity of America's first English settlers. England in the early seventeenth century had a variety of local building styles, and it would seem reasonable to assume that those coming from East Anglia, the Midlands, or the West Country would carry with them to the New World the traditions of their home counties. Only with time would these traditions be transformed into a distinctive American tradition, in both form and regional diversity. A closer look at earlier-seventeenth-century building in New England and the Chesapeake will illustrate this earlier diversity; archaeology plays a critical part in its exposition.

In New England, there are at least two types of buildings that have left no surviving examples. Earthfast construction, so common in the Chesapeake, seems not to have

Figure 10b. Chesapeake end chimney house

been practiced widely in New England. The reasons for this probably relate in large part to both social and economic factors. Unlike Virginians, New Englanders diversified their economy at a very early date, and were engaged in iron production, shipbuilding, mixed crop farming, timber industries, fishing, and even whaling well before mid-century. From the start, the northern colonies were established by families arriving in great numbers, and unlike that of fever-ridden Virginia, New England's climate was most salubrious. People there could expect to live longer than if they had stayed in England. Such a combination of circumstances favored strong economic development almost from the beginning. The absence of a single-crop economy, and the appearance of substantial permanent building at an early date, tell us that New Englanders had a very different

in small things forgotten

outlook on their new home. They were there to stay, to build for a future in their new surroundings. While economic advantages were probably uppermost in the minds of these people, a strong religious motivation, largely lacking in Virginia, only added to their resolve.

But there are a few examples of earthfast buildings to be found in New England. The first of these came to light in 1972. An architect noticed pipestems and pottery fragments in a field in Kingston, Massachusetts, where he was to build a house for a client. He took the artifacts to archaeologists at Plimoth Plantation, where they were seen to be of early-seventeenth-century date. Excavation and deed and title research were begun almost immediately. The property had been granted to Isaac Allerton in 1629. Allerton was the financial agent for the Pilgrim group who settled Plymouth, and one of the more important figures in the establishment of the colony. He moved to Kingston, some three miles distant, shortly after 1629. Excavations showed that he developed the property extensively. Remains of a dwelling house and several outbuildings were located, aligned with a trench that had held a high palisade. The palisade was somewhat of a puzzle, since it was three hundred feet in length but enclosed nothing. We will probably never know why such a one-sided fence was built; the best guess is that when the property was sold in the mid seventeenth century, the palisade was only partially built and the new owner did not care to complete it. To lend support to this explanation, it is clear that the palisade was removed at that time; the dwelling house and outbuildings that had flanked it were razed, and the debris from the dismantling was deposited in the open palisade trench.

The dwelling house had been a small earthfast building, almost square, measuring twenty by twenty-two feet, with a simple hearth, made of cobbles, at one end. The dimensions of this house are very close to those of the first building erected by the Plymouth colonists shortly after landing, a common storehouse twenty feet square. Two other small earthfast buildings have been excavated in New England since 1972, and there is a description of yet another written by William Bradford, who tells us of a hurricane that swept Plymouth Colony in 1635, destroying the trading post at Manomet.

> . . . It took off the borded roof of a house belonging to this plantation at Manamet, and floted it to another place, *the posts still standing in the ground;* and if it had continued long without the shifting of the wind, it is like it would have drouned some parte of the cuntrie."[1]

Another type of house which is known only from archaeology is represented by three sites in the old Plymouth Colony area. These take the form of long, rather narrow houses, with entrances leading directly into the hall. Robert St. George sees houses of this type as typical of the English uplands. He explains such direct access to the hall, the most public social space of the house, as resulting from an economy based primarily on grazing, which led to a very dispersed pattern of settlement, where people seldom saw their neighbors, and had to travel greater distances to visit, thus making the need for privacy minimal.[2] New England sites which have produced evidence of this house type include the Miles Standish and John Alden[3] sites in Duxbury, and the R.M. site in Plymouth, so named for a set of initials scratched on the end of a seal-top spoon, whose former occupant is unknown. The Alden house was ten feet wide and forty feet long, the other two measured sixty by fifteen feet. While the dimensions of the Alden house are smaller than those of the other two, the ratio of length to breadth is the same, of the order of four to one. Interior partition footings in the Standish foundation show the house to have been divided into three rooms; such evidence is lacking for the other two. All three sites date to the 1630s, based on both pipestem and ceramic evidence.

We find in a builder's contract dating to 1638 a description of a house completely unlike any either standing or excavated in New England. One Samuel Symonds of Ipswich, Massachusetts, instructed his house carpenter as follows:

Concerning the frame of the house . . . I am indiferent whether it be 30 foote or 35 foote longe; 16 or 18 foote broade. I would have wood chimnyes at each end, the frames of the chimnyes to be stronger than ordinary, to beare good heavy load of clay for security against fire. You may let the chimnyes by all the breadth of the howse if you thinke good; the

2 lower dores to be in the middle of the howse, one opposite the other. Be sure that all the dorewaies in every place be soe high that any man may goe upright vnder. The staiers I think had best be placed close by the dore. It makes noe great matter though there be noe particion vpon the first flore; if there be, make one biger than the other. For windowes let them not be over large in any roome, & as few as conveniently may be; let all have current shutting draw-windowes, haveing respect both to present & future vse. I thinke to make it a girt howse will make it more chargeable than neede; however the side bearers for the second story, being to be loaden with corne &c. must not be pinned on, but rather eyther lett in to the studds or borne vp with false studds, & soe tenented in at the ends. I leave it to you & the carpenters. In this story over the first, I would have a particion, whether in the middest or over the particion vnder, I leave it. In the garrett noe particion, but let there be one or two lucome windowes, if two, both on one side. I desire to have the sparrs reach downe pretty deep at the eves to preserve the walls the better from the wether, I would have it sellered all over and soe the frame of the howse accordengly from the bottom. I would have the howse stronge in timber, though plaine & well brased. I would have it covered with very good oake-hart inch board, *for the present,* to be tacked

on onely for the present as you tould me. Let the
frame begin from the bottom of the cellar & soe in
the ordinary way vpright, for I can hercafter (to
save the timber within grounde) run vp a thin
brick worke without. I think it best to have the
walls without to be all clapboarded besides the clay
walls. It were not amisse to leave a doreway or two
within the seller, that soe herafter on may make
comings in from without.[4]

Such a house was obviously a substantial structure, and it is
probably no coincidence that it describes a house very like
the one excavated at Flowerdew Hundred, dating to the
second half of the seventeenth century, and associated with
the domestic production of iron.

In the area that once was Massachusetts Bay Colony
there are only a scant dozen houses which predate the middle of the seventeenth century. These all appear to represent yet another type of house, with strong ties to East
Anglia. All are substantial structures, characterized by central chimney placement, flanked by the standard hall-and-
parlor arrangement, with entry through a small interior
porch in front of the chimney. Of these houses, the Jonathan Fairbanks house in Dedham has the distinction of
being the oldest timber-framed structure in the New
World, dated by tree rings and documents to the year 1637.

The Fairbanks house shows its East Anglian derivation not only in the arrangement of rooms, but in a close
parallel with details of framing, including curved wind

braces, as well. The house is also an excellent example of the pattern of growth of seventeenth- and eighteenth-century vernacular American houses. Organic in the extreme, the houses of this early time grew according to need, and in their expansion reflected the development of the families that inhabited them. It is in this seemingly random but truly adaptive kind of accretion that such houses most strongly contrast with the academic structures that come to influence and ultimately replace them. Hugh Morrison makes the comparison succinctly:

> A Gothic building evolved out of the plan, which was controlled by needs, and out of the varied materials employed, which were developed into decorative forms almost adventitiously by the many craftsmen who worked with them. It was not planned, so to speak—it just grew. The great difference between Gothic and Renaissance architecture is not merely a matter of stylistic details, but an essential difference in basic methods and philosophies of building. The one is expressional, the other geometric; Gothic architecture was evolutionary, Renaissance architecture was created.[5]

The Fairbanks house was decidedly evolutionary. It began in 1637 as a typical hall-and-parlor house, with two rooms flanking a central chimney. The hall was somewhat larger than the parlor, and each room had its special functions—as we have seen, technomic in the hall and socio-

in small things forgotten

technic in the parlor. Many see this hall-and-parlor house form as the basic English prototype for all that follows in vernacular American building. It certainly forms the core, or nucleus, for the vast majority of folk buildings in New England. As the seventeenth century went on, lean-to rooms were added to the rear of the Fairbanks house, the parlor and the chamber above were enlarged, a bedroom wing was added to the hall off one end, and a second parlor and bedroom were added to the rear. The resultant floor plan is anything but symmetrical, no more so than the facade of the original house, with two hall windows and one parlor window flanking the entrance. The other early-seventeenth-century houses in the Massachusetts Bay area are roughly similar in plan and pattern of growth.

The diversity in building types in earlier New England is reflected in room naming practices, and the manner in which these changed during the seventeenth century. A study of fifty-eight room-by-room probate inventories from Plymouth Colony, dating from 1633 to 1684, shows a pronounced shift in room naming patterns after 1660.[6] Prior to that date, room names were highly variable, reflecting English room naming practices brought to Plymouth by the early colonists, and the geographic diversity of that population. Many names occur only once, such as dwelling house, a term sometimes used in the Midlands to designate the hall. After 1660, room names become more standardized. The difference is a major one. Prior to 1660, the total number of inventories is only eighteen, yet the sixty-nine rooms represented by these eighteen estates are given thirty-one different names. After 1660, the forty remaining inventories produce only forty-two names for a total of one hundred thirty-nine rooms, a 33 percent reduction. During the later period, three rooms become very common, chamber, parlor, and kitchen. The term "hall" is largely restricted to the earlier period. Halls appear to turn into kitchens as the century progresses. Furthermore, in comparison to halls, kitchens tended to contain a smaller percentage of the total value of the estate, suggesting that the room was becoming more specialized in the direction of food processing and preparation. This change in naming practices would appear to be a function of the emergence of a more American local culture, with a more standardized architectural form accompanied by an increasingly standardized nomenclature for its rooms.

By 1660, great numbers of Anglo-Americans had never seen England, and as we have noted, their lifestyle began to reflect their isolation. This isolation can be seen in certain differences in their houses and the way they were built. To be sure, they remained English in spirit, but it is unlikely that any house constructed in America after the mid seventeenth century would be identified as one built in England if its location were unknown. One factor that led to this divergence in New England was the great supply of wood the colonists found in the New World. By the end of the sixteenth century, wood for building had become a scarce commodity in England. Indeed, the decorative elaboration of Tudor half-timbered structures was ostentation on the part of wealthy builders and owners to show that they could afford such a luxury. In America, virgin forests provided the vernacular builder with more timber than he would ever need, and this difference accounts for some of the distinctiveness of timber frame construction in the colonial world.

By the end of the seventeenth century, New England exhibited marked regionalization in house types; no fewer than four distinctive expressions of house construction could be seen between New Hampshire and the Cape Cod–Rhode Island area. While some of this regional specialization can be attributed to environmental factors, this diversity also attests to the combined effects of isolation from the English homeland and the strong regionalization of cultures, the same factors that produced the varied styles of gravestone art.

Massachusetts Bay Colony followed the English tradition most closely. Those houses that have survived are all based on the hall-and-parlor plan, and the techniques used for framing—cutting of joints, placement of major beams and rafters—follow the English methods closely. Yet even here certain differences emerged. Cecil Hewett has compared houses in Essex, England, with a number of New England examples, primarily in the Massachusetts Bay area.[7] While he has indicated a number of stylistic parallels, in many cases a feature common in America is quite rare in England, so that, statistically at least, the American buildings contrast with their English prototypes. Ground plans are generally similar, but New Englanders invariably place the staircase leading to the upper chambers at the front of the house, while in England it was often placed at the rear. Wooden siding in the form of clapboards is an American trait rarely seen in English houses, probably due to the scarcity of wood in the mother country and the more severe climate of New England, which could well erode the clay walls that the clapboards covered.

Studs (slim vertical wall beams that carry the siding and support the filling of the walls) that run the full distance from foundation to roof in two-story houses are a New England feature seen also in England. Hewett suggests that their adoption was an economy measure, since they do involve less labor than do single-story studs, which must be joined to a major beam running along the line of the second-story floor. Yet in the Fairbanks house, such long studs are compatible with "clamps," horizontal beams attached to the *inside* of the studs, which in turn support the upstairs floor. This is an interesting feature, since in England clamps were used toward the end of the sixteenth century as a part of a great remodeling movement. Old houses in England were without second floors, open in the hall from floor to rafters. In a house already built, the only way one might build in a floor over the hall would be by attaching clamps to the walls on the inside. Yet, at the Fairbanks house, the use of clamped floors was an integral part of the house's original construction. Only one English prototype for this practice is presently known: it is in Essex and occurs on a building of only one and a half stories. An important factor in the framing of the Fairbanks house with two-story studs was the ready availability of trees that would provide such long pieces. Greater access to wood also probably accounts for another difference seen in New England houses: the extensive use of wooden shingles on roofs. Thatch, tile, and slate were the common English roofing materials. All called for heavy roof framing to support their considerable weight. New England houses developed a lighter roof frame almost certainly because of the lighter covering material. The continuous lean-to, an addition to the rear of the house that continues the roof line unbroken nearly to the ground, is a very common New England feature that is uncommon in England. Again, the difference is best explained by the availability of the very long rafters needed to span the distance from roof ridge across the rear room.

Many of the features enumerated are found in folk building over most or all of New England, but they are all present in the Massachusetts Bay area and serve to set apart its vernacular tradition from that of England. Elsewhere in the New England area, even more distinctive features can be seen. In Plymouth Colony by the middle of the seventeenth century, builders had developed a method of siding their houses that became a distinctive trademark of house construction in that area. Rather than attaching siding to studs, beneath which was either clay or brick filling, Plymouth Colony house carpenters clad their houses with vertical planks running the full distance from ground to eaves. Such siding certainly required an ample wood supply. Laths were attached directly to the planks and were plastered in turn.

Vertical plank siding precludes the use of overhangs, or jetties. The jetty was a common feature in English medieval building, that survived into the early seventeenth century. In New England, it was commonly used over most of the Massachusetts Bay area and in Connecticut and Rhode Island. Jetties survive in today's popular architecture as the trademark of "garrison colonial" houses, the name denoting a popular myth as to their use. Many believe that such an overhang allowed the occupants of the house to fire down upon attacking Indians without exposure. Aside from the fact that none of the original jetties has openings through which one could fire a weapon, their use in England for a long time before the founding of the colonies hardly can be explained in this fashion. Other, more reasonable explanations for the jetty include a more efficient use of second-story space in crowded cities and, most reasonable of all, an efficient way to frame a two-story house without unduly weakening the large vertical posts with too many mortises. In any case, jettied houses, common in the Massachusetts Bay area, were virtually unknown in Plymouth Colony, with only one example, the now vanished Allyn house, exhibiting the feature in a nineteenth-century engraving of the building.

In Rhode Island, where quality building stone and ample lime supplies were found, yet another regional style emerged. The so-called "stone-ender" is typical of Rhode Island vernacular building. In striking contrast to the timber-frame tradition of all of Massachusetts, Rhode Island houses were often built with an end chimney and wall entirely of tabular stone. Such a stone wall incorporated the chimney, and in a two-room ground plan, rather than flanking a central fireplace, the rooms were arranged one behind the other, with the hearths side by side rather than back to back, one serving each room, hall, and kitchen.

Houses of logs figure significantly in the popular image of the American past. From Abe Lincoln's childhood in a log cabin to the nineteenth-century adoption of the log cabin as an American symbol, it was long erroneously thought that the earliest houses built by English colonists were also of log. In *The Log Cabin Myth* Harold Shurtleff[8] has effectively disposed of this idea and shows that the first log buildings in America were built by the Swedes in Delaware. The English had never seen such a structure, and upon their arrival in the New World, set about to build the kinds of houses they had known: timber-framed dwellings. Yet, in New Hampshire and Maine, log dwelling houses were built, although in their over-all volume and form they more closely resembled their timber-framed counterparts to the south. Jettied, with steep roofs and sheathed in clapboard, they are hardly distinguishable as log structures until the underlying construction is examined. These buildings date mostly to the turn of the eighteenth century. The appearance of such structures on what was at the time the northern New England frontier must at least in part be attributed to a critical environmental factor, the threat of attack by hostile Indian groups in the area. Yet, in view of their formal similarity to timber-framed houses to the south, in Massachusetts Bay, they can be considered yet another, albeit very specialized, regional type.

The late seventeenth and early eighteenth centuries saw the development of distinctive regional styles in New England, almost certainly due to the combined effects of isolation from the parent architectural tradition and a closer fit with the new environment.

Farther south, in the Chesapeake region, the course of architectural change took a somewhat different direction, and although variations in house form seem more to be a function of various social and economic forces, a distinctively American tradition of building made its appearance there as well. As we have seen, the wholesale adoption of a single-crop economy, tobacco cultivation, also locked the people of the Chesapeake into a single architectural tradition. Earthfast construction was known in England, and carried to the New World by the early settlers. But only in the Chesapeake did it become pervasive. While archaeology shows the same method of construction to appear again and again, the arrangement of the posts which supported the house and framed wooden chimneys shows a variety of floor plans. Both central chimney placement and chimneys on either or both ends of the house can be seen. Cellars are not always present; those that were built range from shallow dirt-floored root cellars to deeper brick-lined and -floored affairs, occupying as much as half of the space beneath the house. Although clear evidence for internal partitions is usually lacking, it is safe to assume that any

in small things forgotten

earthfast house large enough to have been divided internally would have been of the hall-and-parlor type.

One type of early-seventeenth-century earthfast house encountered in the Chesapeake has important social implications.[9] Known as a cross passage house, it is characterized by a floor plan consisting of a hall and parlor separated from another set of rooms by a transverse passage running from front to rear (see Figure 11). Such an arrangement made it possible to house servants in immediate proximity to the hall, a convenient arrangement for an agricultural household. Cross passage houses were seen as appropriate by people of all economic levels earlier in the seventeenth century, but by the century's close they had disappeared. We shall see that this change in house form is the consequence of a rather complex set of changes in social relationships between servants and their masters. Indeed, Robert St. George has put forth an explanation of all earthfast building which turns on the nature of social interaction in preindustrial communities.[10] In examining account books kept by two Connecticut craftsmen, a carpenter and a mason, St. George was struck by the fact that both men spent a disproportionate amount of time in maintaining their work after it was completed, more than the income from such repairs would suggest. From this and similar examples of other craftsmen, particularly thatchers, he concluded that mutual maintenance was a significant part of a set of reciprocal relationships that lent coherence to a community in preindustrial times. In this light, the earthfast building functioned to maintain social relationships between mem-

Figure 11. Cross passage house

bers of the community. One need not pay a large sum for the construction of a structure that would be nearly maintenance free, because in exchange for other services rendered to the house carpenter, repair would be forthcoming at no monetary cost. A kind of "you scratch my back and I'll scratch yours" approach to maintenance existed, so that one was assured of having houses and equipment in reasonable working order with no monetary transactions involved.

in small things forgotten

Does this make sense in a world where labor was costly? It does, for the labor which required capital investment was not that which was needed to repair wagon wheels, patch a thatched roof, or replace a rotted post in a dwelling house. These are occasional needs, met by specific members of the community, not involving a constant day-to-day attending of a crop from which one hopes to make one's fortune. Earthfast construction not only makes sense in terms of spending priorities in a situation where most investment must be committed to raising tobacco; it also provides the assurance that one's equipment will be maintained without any significant cash outlay for the service.

Building in brick was practiced in the Chesapeake, but only rarely. The most notable example of substantial brick construction of houses, or at least footings, is found at Jamestown, Virginia's first capital, where the assembly tried without success to promote this kind of building. Virginia's oldest surviving seventeenth-century house, Bacon's Castle, is a large brick house, cross-shaped, with a porch tower at the front and a stair tower at the rear. Its architectural detailing, especially the chimneys and gables, has a strong Jacobean flavor. Constructed in 1665, Bacon's Castle is but one of only two surviving seventeenth-century buildings in Virginia. Impermanent construction combined with the ravages of termites have effectively erased all of the others, leaving the Chesapeake region without the wonderful architectural legacy that is New England's, literally hundreds of surviving seventeenth-century frame houses.

Lacking such buildings in the Chesapeake, we must

turn to other evidence for insights regarding changes in architecture in that region during the seventeenth century. In an important study of room-by-room inventories from seventeenth- and early-eighteenth-century Virginia, Dell Upton has shown how the size of houses changed as a result of changes in the social order.[11] The successful production of tobacco requires a substantial labor force, and this need was met in the Chesapeake at first by indentured servants. These were people who agreed to serve a master for an agreed-upon amount of time in exchange for passage to America and maintenance in the form of food, lodging, and clothing for the period of their indenture. Later, these servants would be replaced by Africans, who were arriving in the region in increasingly large numbers as the seventeenth century drew to a close. The manner in which laborers, either indentured servants or slaves, were housed changed after mid-century, and the probate inventories show how this transformation was brought about. Upton's conclusions were based on a study of room-by-room inventories taken between 1640 and 1720. Most of the houses represented were small, one to three rooms in size. But when one group of houses is considered, those of eight to eleven rooms, a surprising pattern of change over time can be seen. These large houses increase in number, reaching a peak in 1680, but then become fewer, returning to their 1640 number by 1720. Upton explains this pattern as resulting from increasing conflict between masters and servants beginning in the 1660s. Prior to that time, most servants lived in the same house as their masters, either in a cross

in small things forgotten

passage arrangement or in upstairs chambers, so that the increase in the number of large houses reflects the increasing number of people who could afford servants. The growing strain on the social contract between masters and servants is witnessed by a sharp increase in servant-master litigation in the court records, with servants claiming a breach of contract and their masters feeling that they were not receiving the services to which they were entitled. The reaction of the masters to this conflict was to remove the servants to separate quarters at some distance from the house. So while the amount of living space for both groups remained essentially the same, that space formerly given over to housing servants in the main house was no longer needed, with the resultant reduction in numbers of rooms. This is the pattern of building layout that was to become standard over the South during the eighteenth century, with slaves replacing indentured servants in separate quarters. But the arrangement predates the full-blown institution of slavery, so that one group of people simply replaced another. A contemporary description of these late-seventeenth-century communities makes the point quite clearly:

> Some people in this country are comfortably housed . . . Whatever their rank, and I know not why, they build only two rooms with some closets on the ground floor, and two rooms in the attic above; but they build several like this, according to their means. They build also a separate kitchen, a separate house for the Christian slaves, some for

the negro slaves, and several to dry the tobacco, so that when you come to the home of a person of some means, you think you are entering a fairly large village.[12]

By the early eighteenth century, New England and the Chesapeake each show a rather standardized form of house to be typical of the respective regions. In New England, the central chimney house with rearward projecting kitchen became more and more commonplace, and in the Chesapeake, houses of single-room depth and end chimneys predominate, usually two-room buildings arranged in the standard hall-and-parlor layout. Both types were present in New England and the Chesapeake from the start, but over time, houses arranged in these two different plans came to be typical of their regions, and can be seen today by the hundreds in both places. It has been argued that these two house plans are indicative of a kind of environmental adaptation. In New England, so the reasoning goes, a centrally located chimney would form a heating core for the house, especially if it were constructed of heat-retaining masonry, as these were. Conversely, locating the chimneys at the ends of houses in the hot, humid Tidewater region would dissipate the heat generated in the summer by the constant need for cooking fires. The separate kitchen, common in the South, is but a logical extension of such an arrangement. However, such an explanation runs the risk of being an oversimplified one, based on modern reasoning applied to houses of the eighteenth century, while not taking into account all of the factors that might have led to the differences. Certainly in the case of the Chesapeake elite, Fraser Neiman sees this explanation as "an example of environmental determinism at its worst."[13] He correctly states that archaeological evidence shows that interior porch entry central chimney houses were among the most common forms used by the gentry of the Chesapeake during the seventeenth century. Their chimneys were mostly framed with timber and covered with clay daub. By the time end chimneys of brick make their appearance among the Chesapeake gentry, cooking had already been shifted in location from the main house to a separate kitchen, yet one more instance of the spatial separation between masters and servants or slaves.

While American vernacular housing had become a tradition recognizably different from that of its Old World roots, beneath it all there remained something distinctively English—a way of organizing space and creating livable volumes. Henry Glassie's analysis of folk building in middle Virginia shows clearly the power of the mind-set expressed in every house in New England as well as those in the middle-Atlantic colonies even a century later. We have seen that language can be considered as an aspect of material culture. Certainly in terms of the fundamental structure of language, a sound argument can be put forth in favor of an essential identity. Glassie has formulated a grammar that accounts for the pattern of folk building he observed in middle Virginia.

A grammar, in linguistics, is a set of rules for the

formulation of utterances in such a way as to be mutually accepted by all speakers of a language. Likewise, a grammar can be thought of as a set of rules for the creation of artifacts mutually accepted by the members of the culture producing them. Such rules definitely exist, even if they cannot be explicitly stated by their users. Otherwise there would be no consistency in design traditions or in methods of creating houses, tools, or weapons. On occasion, anthropologists have been able to determine such rules for material culture production. A notable example is Lila O'Neale's study of Yurok-Karok basketry, in which basketmakers commented on each other's work: what was wrong and what was right about it.[14] From her interviews, O'Neale was able to set down a number of rules that share all their principles with grammatical rules. Certain materials were not to be used with certain others in making a basket; it just wasn't "right." The principle of harmony between design elements around the rim of a basket hat and those in the main decorative field is strikingly similar to the grammatical rule in English of agreement between subject and verb.

It is likewise with vernacular housing, as Glassie shows us. His grammar is a *generative,* or *transformational,* one, whereby a number of basic forms can be shown to be combined according to a set of transformations to generate all culturally acceptable house forms. As he has prepared it, the grammar applies only to the houses from which it was developed, but within that group of houses, a relatively

in small things forgotten

small set of rules, nine subdivided sets, accounts for the complete generation of the folk house of middle Virginia.

In arriving at the grammar for the Virginia tradition, Glassie has penetrated deeply into the folk builder's mind, and made explicit what each builder carried with him in an unconscious, implicit way. At his deepest level of abstraction, that of the geometric entity from which all further generation of forms derives, we see the fundamental unit that also ties together all of Anglo-America's vernacular buildings and relates them to their English counterparts. The unit in question is a square, ideally sixteen feet on a side. Glassie suggests that this volume is one in which an Anglo-American feels most comfortable. Sixteen feet is the common dimensional denominator of almost every house erected before the advent of academic architectural forms in time or space. Glassie sees it as a multiple of the cubit (eighteen inches), and his measurements of many houses support this proposition. Yet, there are cubit multiples other than sixteen (or sixteen and a half, to be precise) feet, and the sixteen-foot unit pervades Anglo-American folk housing. Rooms tend to be sixteen feet square, chimney sections of houses eight feet (half the unit) wide, and ceilings usually in excess of seven feet.

So it seems that when a house grew according to the needs of its occupants, such growth proceeded in volumes based on the sixteen-foot module in a decidedly nonsymmetrical way. While symmetry was not a primary consideration, we can see by looking at the plans and facades of these buildings, there had to be some governing set of implicit concerns guiding their growth. Most important, these concepts were those of the builder, who was intimately a part of the society for which the house was produced, and as such closely reflect that society's values.

At about the same time that Boston stonecutters were carving their first cherubs atop gravestones, the first Georgian houses were being built in the city. America's first Georgian building was the Foster-Hutchinson house, built in Boston in 1688. It is known today only from an 1836 engraving and a brief description by a British officer who witnessed its looting and partial destruction by a mob protesting the Stamp Act in 1765. It seems to have been the embodiment of the Georgian style and greatly resembled buildings designed by Inigo Jones in England. Other houses followed in Boston and other wealthy port cities as the eighteenth century began, and soon the impact of academic design was being felt throughout the colonial world.

The Georgian style, which so influenced the form of Anglo-American building, had its roots in the Renaissance. Inigo Jones is credited with its introduction to England, and from there, after a period of development in the seventeenth century, it was introduced into the colonies at that century's end. Strictly formal in its adaptation of classical architectural detail, the Georgian was rigidly symmetrical and bilateral, both in facade and floor plan. The classical Georgian house has a central hall that separates two sets of two rooms each. From the front, it exhibits strict bilaterality and balance: a central doorway flanked by paired evenly spaced windows and a central second-floor window directly over the door. These windows have multiple panes and sliding sashes, in contrast to the leaded casement windows of medieval type used in early vernacular houses. Doors are paneled, with porticoes in classical design. The entire configuration is profoundly different from that of the houses built before its advent.

The adoption of Georgian building in the colonies came about in several ways. The wealthier men in the cities, often trained to some extent in architecture in England, were both conversant with the style and had the means to have it created in America. The number of skilled craftsmen required to create such houses was steadily increasing in the eighteenth century, and some of them had the necessary experience and familiarity with the design. Perhaps the most important single factor in the introduction of the Georgian style into America was the large number of architectural books that appeared on the scene from the late seventeenth century onward. Of two types, volumes on the classical orders of architecture and carpenters' handbooks, together they enabled a person of means to work with experienced help to construct such a grand edifice. The fact that the houses' forms were derived from books rather than from the mind of a folk builder is what probably sets the academic Georgian apart from the vernacular tradition so clearly. Recalling both Gowans' and Morrison's descriptions of this new order of building, we can see that design now overrode function. So much did this occur, that in at least one case the symmetry of the facade was preserved even though an interior partition abutted a window, rendering it useless.

Since the Georgian style was ordered by a careful consideration of academic treatises on classical architectural forms, and since this consideration was often conveyed to the builders of the houses through a limited number of books, it is not surprising that we see an increasing similarity in houses over all of Anglo-America as the eighteenth century progresses. Not that there were not slight regional variations; New England favored wood, as before, while brick was more commonly used farther south; the South employed hip roofs more than the North. But in contrast to the extreme regional variation of the pre-Georgian tradition, the similarities far exceeded the differences. Such broad similarity, with its origin among the urban elite, is one more hallmark of the re-Anglicized popular culture of America on the eve of the Revolution.

The new, academic architectural form was not without its impact on the earlier, vernacular tradition. One style did not simply replace the other, and houses of the older type continued to be built until the end of the eighteenth century or later. In time, the earlier tradition took on aspects of the new. Sometimes this modification was more thorough than a simple transfer of discrete elements. In its simplest form, an attempt was made to create a Georgianized facade for an otherwise pre-Georgian building, almost as if the owners desired to present a more contemporary face to the world while retaining their comfortable older house behind it.

The Mott farmhouse, in Portsmouth, Rhode Island, is an example of this process (see Figure 2b). This house was developed in a series of builds beginning in the late seventeenth century and lasting into the nineteenth. During this time, it was the residence of the same family, the Motts, who acquired the property in 1639 and did not leave it until the end of the 1800s. The first house built on the property no longer existed on the site in 1972, when the entire structure was systematically dismantled. The late-seventeenth-century house formed the core of the old farmhouse, and when first built it was probably a stone-end house with a jetty on the opposite, gable end. In the middle of the eighteenth century, the house was remodeled, and in the process the facade was given certain features that have a Georgian flavor but only in a most superficial way. The end chimney was removed and replaced by a central chimney, which stood between the original hall and a new, two-story addition on the opposite side. The ridge line of the roof of this addition ran at right angles to that of the first build. The jetty was removed at this time, making the facade an even plane, and the roof of the first house was covered by a continuation of the roof of the addition. However, the builders simply covered the end of the old roof opposite the addition to conform to its original slope, creating a final roof shape that was hipped at one end only.

This asymmetrical roof line almost certainly came about more through expediency than from a commitment to any stylistic concept; although the hip roof is a Georgian feature, and rarely seen on earlier buildings, its presence on only one end is a violation of the severe Georgian symmetry. The same applies to the facade of the house. The placement of the windows in the new addition, and their relationship to the windows of the old, and to the entrance, follows the Georgian layout in scheme, but the windows are situated in a way that makes us believe that the builder was only faintly conversant with the formal rules of Georgian architecture. It is as if, in remodeling the house, the builder brought to his job only a passing awareness of the new style; the manner in which he employed it reflects the imperfection and distortion in his perceptions.

The Mott house represents the impact of Georgian design on vernacular building at its most imperfect and slightest degree. More commonly, older house facades were styled by replacing the old casement windows with the new sliding sashes, adding a more classical door, and otherwise adding details that did not alter the basic form of the house. Glassie's grammar for folk housing in Virginia includes a set of rules that generate Georgian-like buildings, but, again, they do not conform to the full canons of the style. In this part of the South, a common vernacular house type is one room deep and two rooms long, a basic hall-and-parlor plan. Two-story houses of this type were built under the impact of the Georgian tradition, with a central hall that forms the front, and while they exhibit all the characteristics of the style, the single-room depth is retained. Again, the house displays a full Georgian facade, but in its ground plan it is still a pre-Georgian building. In their ambiguity and their accommodation of two somewhat conflicting values, these "hybrid" houses are strongly reminiscent of the gravestones carved in rural New England in the mid-eighteenth century. In both cases, there is a mutual accommodation between older and newer traditions, the older reflecting deeply held and comfortable values, the newer the face that is presented to the world. Vinal's "bird" skulls embody the old death's-head symbolism and at the same time smile out at the world in much the same way as do the cherubs of contemporary urban and elite Boston.

One of the more striking differences between the old, medieval-derived building tradition and the classical style that influenced and replaced it is in the relationship among the individuals, their family, their house, and their community. A New England seventeenth-century house provided space that was corporately used. We have seen that the foodways of the pre-Georgian period were characterized by sharing of utensils. In a similar way, space was shared by all the members of the residential group, and rooms were the containers for tightly knit groups of people. Privacy as we know it could not have existed, and the separation of various activities was far less. Room-by-room inventories tell us that a variety of food and artifact production took place within the same space, as did other, purely social functions. A visitor entering such a house either stepped directly into this activity or was separated from it only by a small porch (see Figure 12a).

Glassie contrasts this with the visitor's experience upon entering a Georgian house, where one was welcomed by an unheated central hall, showing only doors behind

Figure 12a. Seventeenth-century hall-and-parlor house

which the family carried out its daily functions (see Figure 12b). The higher degree of spatial specialization in such a house not only isolated the family members from the outside but also from each other; clearly the result is the individualization of living space. Of course, much of this separation can come about only in a structure complex enough

in small things forgotten

Figure 12b. Georgian-derived vernacular house

to permit it. Nonetheless, a house considered both expensive and adequate to the needs of its inhabitants in the seventeenth century was less divided than was its eighteenth-century equivalent.

So it is that with the coming of the Georgian style the

characteristics of our third period, already observed in very different contexts, can be seen to be operative in housing. The earliest houses show strong ties to the English homeland, and in time become more American and more regionally diverse. In all of this time, they are organic, corporate, and exhibit a growth that is sensitive to the needs of the family unit. Not only is the Georgian style an imposed order, it is totally mechanical in its integration, and its characteristic balance, symmetry, and order speak to us in the same way as do individualized graves and markers, and matched individual sets of china. And in every instance, the new order had its origins among the urban sophisticates, from whom it was passed slowly to their rural neighbors. By the time of the American Revolution, large numbers of Anglo-Americans partook of a new outlook on the world, acquired from an England under the impact of the Renaissance.

6

small things remembered

The three categories of material culture we have considered thus far—ceramics, houses, and gravestones—have given us some special insights into the Anglo-American experience since the early seventeenth century. Indeed, they are the most useful for this purpose, for each has some special characteristic not found in most other material categories. Ceramics were common: they are a constant component of all archaeological assemblages, and their use relates directly to a universal human experience, subsistence. Houses, as the structures within which so much of our existence in a variety of activities is spent, naturally relate to that existence in a sensitive way. And when we combine the archaeological evidence of early building with those houses that have survived, we have a large body of information with which to work. Gravestones also attest to a universal of human life, the leave-taking of it, and those of early New England are so numerous and so subject to controlled study that they, too, permit a very detailed analysis in terms of the culture that produced them. All three, then, inform us in terms of the people who used them; all three provide direct reflections of those people's lives.

Unfortunately, such is not so with many other kinds of artifacts. Furniture, the subject of so much interest in the study of the decorative arts, is less useful in answering the kinds of questions we have asked. Except for its mention in inventories, never in the kind of detail we need, early American furniture has survived without a behavioral context. Save for the hardware with which it is assembled, furniture cannot be recovered archaeologically, so that its association with the larger material culture system of which it was a part cannot be thus determined. If we could have been so fortunate as to have observed furniture in its living setting, its mode of use would support many of the conclusions we have drawn. The few phenomena that can be observed are suggestive.

The use of chairs by the simple folk of England for the purely technomic purpose of sitting began in the very late sixteenth and early seventeenth centuries. Prior to that time, chairs were rare, and households that possessed them at all frequently had only one. Chairs, more than any other item of furniture, had, from ancient times, a strong ideotechnic dimension, in that they were associated with leadership and authority. The use of the chair in the household reflected its use in government. As the ruler was enthroned before his court and kingdom, so was the husbandman enthroned within his household. Others sat on stools, chests, settles, benches, cushions, or rush-covered floor. Certainly, the straight-backed, flat-wooden-seated armchair that so frequently constituted the household's single chair was not more comfortable than these—in some cases perhaps less so. Although the small size of the sample makes meaningful statistical comparison impossible, the impression gained from Plymouth's earliest inventories, dating from the 1630s, is that, per capita, chairs were fewer in that colony than in contemporary England. But most inventories contain at least one chair, again suggesting the strength of the artifact's symbolic dimension.

When chairs started to become more numerous on estate inventories, both in England and Anglo-America, they appear to have been of diverse varieties within a household. A single room might contain: "wainscott chair," "joined chair," "leather-covered chair," "wicker chair," "table-chair." Within the classical furniture traditions that accompany the Georgian architectural style, chairs were made in matched sets, as were plates. Moreover, the compartmentalization of the house and separation of household activities required an individual group of chairs for each room, whereas before, most, if not all, the chairs were located in the hall.

In early Plymouth and elsewhere, bedsteads were also not universal, and an estate often had none. In both cases, while sharing of such furniture in an earlier time cannot be proved, not every member of the household was accounted for by an individual, similar piece of furniture, a pattern that certainly appears later.

During the second period, furniture, like houses, exhibits a strong English flavor and spirit but yet is regionally distinct and unmistakably American. This observation is based on surviving pieces, of course, which are not truly representative of the entire social range. Still, carved and painted chests from Connecticut are easily distinguished from those made in Plymouth Colony, and both from their Massachusetts Bay counterparts. In the eighteenth century, under the impact of classical styles, American furniture, like Georgian houses, becomes less diverse in form, although even at that time a high-boy or a clock from Philadelphia was still somewhat different stylistically from similar pieces made in Newport.

In the case of most tools and implements, the information content is even lower, either because not enough has been learned about them or because they are so rarely available. This is due either to genuine rarity or to a failure to identify them for what they are.

Cutlery and tableware do exhibit certain changes that indirectly relate to changes in foodways. In seventeenth-century England, knives used in food consumption had blades with pointed ends, which served to convey food to the mouth. Forks were not present at the time. They were an Italian invention and did not become popular among simpler folk in England until the mid seventeenth century at the earliest. But, in America, their appearance was much later. Although Governor Winthrop of Massachusetts is known to have owned one—it survives today—forks do not appear in archaeological sites until the early eighteenth

in small things forgotten

century. The first mention of a fork in the Plymouth Colony area probate inventories is in 1721, in the estate of a wealthy gentleman in Marshfield, but significant numbers of forks do not show up in these records until the second half of the century. When forks appeared in quantities in England, knives changed in shape, and rounded blade ends replaced the pointed ones, since forks had assumed the function of the pointed blade. However, since most knives were made in England, and the fork appeared later in America, this relationship did not prevail in the New World.

Using a round-ended knife and not having a fork, one would either have made considerable use of the fingers conveying solid foods to the mouth or made do with a spoon. This raises an interesting, if conjectural, point. Americans often comment that Europeans use their forks "upside down." In fact, by the simple rule of priority and majority, it is we Americans who are "upside down." Since we did not learn to use forks until some time after the ends of knives were rounded, the change in the manner of food conveyance was not directly from knife tip to fork tine, as it was in England. The only intermediate utensil available was the spoon; one could cut food and transfer it to the spoon bowl. If even one generation used knife and spoon in this manner, the fork, upon its belated appearance, would be used in a manner similar to the spoon. Which is precisely the way we use it today. Yet, in its function of anchoring food for cutting, the fork is held curve down; it is turned over while transferring the food from the plate to the mouth. This distinctive way of using the knife, fork, and spoon came into existence during the late seventeenth and early eighteenth centuries, and thus is one more American idiosyncrasy arising from isolation during that period.

Moving to the foodstuffs consumed with knife, fork, and spoon, we see another pattern of change consistent with those already observed. Medieval cookery was marked by the combining of all manner of foodstuffs into stews, pottages, and other exotic mixtures. This characteristic it shares with most of the world's cuisines; mixed dishes are far more common than separate servings of the individual components of a meal. Such cookbooks as Gervase Markham's *The English Housewife,* published in England in 1615, tell us that mixed dishes were typical of English cookery at the time of the colonization of America. However, by the end of the eighteenth century, the kind of meals we are accustomed to today had become commonplace. This change is but another instance of the shift from a world view of a corporate nature to one that places great emphasis on the individual.

The ideal American meal of meat, potato, and vegetable is not only tripartite in its structure but very mechanical, while a seventeenth-century pottage in which all were combined was both organic and corporate in form. Those paper plates we buy at the supermarket may be divided into three sections because of a very deep tripartite mental structure. Their structural similarity to a Georgian facade may be much more than coincidental. If so, the familiar compartmented baby plate would impress such separateness upon us at a very early point in our enculturation.

This change in food preparation is shown by the animal bone found on sites of the seventeenth and eighteenth centuries. In the late eighteenth century, a rather abrupt change occurred in the method of cutting up the carcass of an animal into portions that can be cooked. The earlier method, which is contemporary with the period of mixed cooking, was marked by chopping of the bone, probably with an ax. Such a quartering method did not permit the closest control over the size of the resulting portions, nor did it permit the production of small cuts, such as chops, steaks, or short ribs. Hacking a carcass into rather large chunks produced large pieces of meat that could be roasted and then corporately consumed, or cooked in a stew in which the meat would cook from the bone and blend with the other ingredients. This quartering technique was replaced by the use of saws to divide up the animal. Saws were a part of the tool kit of every American from the time of the colonies' beginning, but were used to cut meat only after the late eighteenth century. A saw can produce servings controlled as to size. Unless there was a great need for such individualized servings, sawing would be unnecessary, but given the discrete serving of various foodstuffs, carefully individualized portions of meat would be highly desirable.

The disposal of refuse is one of our most unconscious acts: while we might suspect some hidden motive in the way a court clerk recorded the disposition of a case or a diarist described his neighbors, it is most unlikely that in removing food remains, broken dishes, and other debris from a household, people were making any conscious statement about themselves or others. Yet, in the changing nature of trash disposal since the seventeenth century, our ancestors have once again informed us of the way in which their view of the world was changing.

A hallmark of archaeological sites of the seventeenth century is the broadcast sheet of refuse that surrounds them. Apparently, all waste materials were simply thrown out, and often at what to us would be an alarmingly short distance from the door. Such a practice probably had its practical value: pigs and chickens foraging around the house could eat what was edible, leaving the rest to become covered slowly with soil. Almost any site that dates to a time prior to the mid eighteenth century shows such a refuse-disposal pattern. It works a hardship on the archaeologist, for the artifacts included in the refuse have been trod upon repeatedly and reduced to very small pieces. Occasionally, we encounter a shallow, irregular pit that contains refuse, but these were almost certainly dug fortuitously either by children, chickens, or pigs. Deep, structured trash pits were not a part of the pre-Georgian New Englander's world.

Shortly after 1750, this practice changed. In its place, people dug square pits, often as deep as seven feet, which received the refuse produced by their households. Such pits are very common on sites of this time, and some may have served some other purpose originally: as privies or for storage. But a number of them seem intentionally to have been made for the disposal of trash. Their contents include artifacts and food remains. Since disposal seems to have been directly into the pits, preservation is much better than is that of artifacts randomly scattered over the site, and it is not unusual to recover large numbers of fully restorable bottles, plates, cups, and saucers.[1]

A simple explanation for such a change in refuse disposal practices would be that they represent a correlate of population increase and concentration. After all, in a built-up area, random scattering of refuse could be very noisome and might well cause the neighbors to complain. Yet this does not seem to be the case, for in the waterfront area of Salem, Massachusetts, where there was a heavy concentration of building from the seventeenth century, in the center of Plymouth, where a comparable population density was not achieved until later, and at the Fairbanks house in Dedham, which even today is in a less settled area, the change from scattered refuse disposal to burial in pits occurs at almost the same time: in the second half of the eighteenth century.

Once again, this change may reflect a deeper order of things. After all, such precise and neat handling of one of life's less useful and valuable things suggests almost a compulsion to order. The old adage "a place for everything, and everything in its place" could well be of eighteenth-century coinage, so well does it express the compulsive order that Americans brought to their material world at that time.

By now we have considered a wide variety of material culture. In ways great or small, gravestones, grave pits, houses, refuse, cuts of meat, recipes, ceramics, furniture, and cutlery inform us that a great change was worked between 1760 and 1800 on the worldview of most of Anglo-America. So constant is the time of occurrence, that with some practices, such as refuse disposal, we are strongly inclined to explain the change in these terms, even if the specifics of the example itself are not greatly detailed and explicit. The change must have been at a very deep level of the Anglo-American mind, since it is so abstract as to manifest itself on the surface in so many different ways. The entire social order must have been similarly affected. For example, Anne Yentsch has discovered that in Plymouth Colony the first-generation settlers practiced marriage patterns identical to those of England.[2] But during the period from 1660 through 1760, they developed a different marriage system, characterized by brother-sister marriage in pairs: a brother and sister of one family would marry a sister and brother of another. Such a pattern would strengthen the solidarity of the local community and may have contributed, however slightly, to social isolation. More important, it is a distinctively Anglo-American folk practice, best explained by the isolation of its practitioners from the mother country. After 1760, the marriage system reverted to that of England and has remained so to this day.

in small things forgotten

In a few remote pockets of America, the old agrarian lifeway, with its organic solidarity, was preserved to a remarkable extent. In the hollows of the mountain South, the traditional lifeways were preserved up until the coming of rural electrification, in the early twentieth century. Subsistence farming was the primary economic base, and barter was the standard form of exchange. The population was small and rather evenly dispersed over the countryside. Ways of cooking food, building houses, cultivating the land, singing songs, weaving cloth—in short, of making one's way through life—were directly related to and descended from the English tradition which lay at their roots. In its isolation, this part of America went its way with relatively little influence from the vast changes being worked on the culture of its more cosmopolitan neighbors. Electricity changed the traditional lifeways. Mills were established; towns grew in size, and there was a large migration from the countryside to the new jobs available in the towns. Radios became popular and were among the major factors in breaking down the isolation and bringing the outside world in.

The end result was the imposition of the new on the old, and the effect is much like the changes worked on Joshua Hempstead's Essex County gravestone designs when they were introduced into Connecticut. The sequence seems to have been repeated, but at an accelerated rate. Consider the changes that took place in traditional music in the mountain South after the turn of the twentieth century.

Eric Davidson and Paul Newman have analyzed the

social history of traditional music in southwestern Virginia, and their research provides us with a good understanding of how and why the forms have changed.[3] The people of the Appalachian highlands in Virginia and West Virginia are largely descendants of Britishers who moved into the area before the American Revolution. With them they carried the old way of English life which we have observed in the material culture of New England, and their music was no exception. Field work in the area by Cecil Sharp and Olive Campbell in the early twentieth century established that there was a remarkable survival of English ballads and tunes. Two centuries earlier, it must have been much stronger.

The main musical instrument on which dance tunes were played was the fiddle, an instrument that saw similar popularity in England and that must have been brought to America with the first settlers; one appears in a probate inventory during the first half of the seventeenth century in Plymouth. Even today, old fiddlers play tunes that make use of a technique known as "double stopping," in which two strings are bowed at the same time, with one acting as a drone string. A drone, musically, is a single sustained note without change. We are most familiar with the drone effect in music of the bagpipe, in which two pipes act as drones, played by the inflated bags, and the third is noted, like a whistle. Bagpipes and fiddles played with drones produce a musical form that is quite archaic, typical of the Middle Ages. Another southern musical instrument, the dulcimer, is also characterized by drone strings. This instrument,

in small things forgotten

probably a derivative of a German instrument known as a *Scheitholt*, found its way into the mountains probably in the late eighteenth century and is most frequently used in accompanying ballads. It usually has three or four strings, two or three of which are tuned in such a way that they are never noted but produce a harmonic drone along with the melody, which is picked out on the one or two other strings.

Fiddles then were played in a style both traditional and similar to that used in England. Even the manner of holding the instrument may reflect its traditional English origin. The medieval way of playing the fiddle, against the chest rather than beneath the chin, is seen even today in the southern highlands, and while the resemblance could be accidental, it seems more likely that there is also a kenesic conservatism in mountain fiddle playing.

Ballads are traditionally sung *a capella* today and were in the past. Taken with the dance tunes, these songs probably formed the musical repertoire of the first settlers in the mountains, and more closely resemble the music of the England from which they came than did the distinctively American musical forms that superseded them as the nineteenth century progressed. Evidence, not only in instrument form and use but also in repertoire—ballads such as "Barbara Allen" and "Butcher's Boy" and such tunes as "Soldier's Joy" and "Devil's Dream"—indicates a period sometime in the eighteenth century when southern mountain music shared greatly with the British Isles. As such it conforms to our first period, for identical reasons. Similarly, once isolated, it began to change, and in this change to diverge from its parent tradition. We would expect a distinctive Anglo-American musical tradition to emerge, and it is precisely this which is remembered and indulged in by the oldest living informants in the area today.

There is some uncertainty as to just when the five-string banjo made its way into the southern mountains. Most scholars agree that it was there prior to the Civil War; whenever it arrived, it worked a major change on the form of the music in the area. The banjo is of African origin, and in its earliest form lacked frets and had a head formed by stretching skin over a gourd. The distinctive fifth string, a drone, was added during the first half of the nineteenth century, and the instrument incorporated into the mountain tradition was of this type. Both in the manner of playing the instrument in the mountains—picked downward with the fingers—and in the way it is tuned, the banjo is used in a very different way from that in the parallel American minstrel tradition. For these reasons, its use in the mountains is quite distinctive. In its adaptation to mountain music, it was played in such a way as to parallel the melodic line of the fiddle almost identically. So close is the fit that Davidson and Newman believe that its use in the mountains was almost exclusively with a fiddle, to form what is Anglo-America's most musical group, the string band. They call attention to an asymmetry between fiddle and banjo repertoires, with almost all banjo tunes having a fiddle counterpart but only about half of the fiddle tunes played on the banjo.

The result—the banjo-fiddle string band—is traditional in musical form, and intensely corporate in its production. So much is the latter so that interviewed musicians state that a tune played without an accompanying banjo is only "half a tune."[4] To produce one cultural whole requires the activity of two individuals. The tunes played also show their medieval heritage, since they are almost without exception played in modal scales, which use as few as five notes, in contrast with most Renaissance-derived music, based on the octave in major and minor keys.

The functional aspect of fiddle-banjo music underscores its corporate aspect. It was used to accompany social dancing by groups and served the fundamental purpose of expediting an otherwise onerous co-operative work project. Dances were held in conjunction with house raisings, husking bees, and co-operative harvest activities. The musicians sat down to play and would play in unison throughout a long number, never taking a solo break. Such music was technomic in its direct role of accomplishing a task, the production of music for a social occasion. Some of the dance tunes had words, but these were sung when the musician felt like it and perhaps for only one verse and refrain during a total performance lasting ten to fifteen minutes. No introduction or coda marked the beginning or end of a tune, which usually consisted of two parts, each repeated twice. This corporate social role of dance music in the mountains was the most susceptible to outside influence and change, and with the population shifts of the early twentieth century, the occasions that required such music became fewer and fewer. Yet it lasted long enough to be within the memory of those still alive. If it began sometime in the mid nineteenth century, then we can see a second period in musical development, closely parallel to that period a century earlier that saw similar traditions develop in Anglo-America under conditions of isolation, but lasting until the first years of the present century.

However belatedly the mountain South was brought into the larger world, which had a different design for life and its arrangement, once in, we find a striking similarity between the way its music changed and the way the material world of the rest of Anglo-America was transformed. With electricity came radios; with industry, young people ventured farther from home and the old order changed. Influences from black music including jazz and blues filtered in; the guitar made its appearance for the first time, requiring a seven-note scale and obviating the necessity to tune the banjo in a variety of ways to match different modal scales; singing songs in parts and in harmony became popular. After a period of transition, a new, very mechanical musical form appeared, known today as bluegrass music. Bluegrass can be interpreted as the result of imposing the new American worldview on the old musical order. It was originated by Bill Monroe, a Kentucky mandolin player whose Bluegrass Boys at one time included Earl Scruggs, credited with the invention of a very different, nontraditional banjo style, "Scruggs picking," that uses three fingers. Bluegrass became popular in the 1940s and today is primarily an urban style, played and enjoyed over much of America. Its style and widespread occurrence mark it as a popular cultural form. Lyrics of many bluegrass songs talk about leaving the old home place, of missing the country, and other expressions of lonely sentiment for a life that once was but is no more. But it is in its structure and function that bluegrass music both contrasts strongly with the older traditional style and best reflects the changes going on in Anglo-America.

Bluegrass is a performing style of music. It is listened to, not danced to. Instrumentation can include guitar, banjo, fiddle, mandolin, and acoustic bass fiddle. Tunes range from those taken from the traditional repertoire to purely popular compositions, either written expressly for the style or borrowed from elsewhere including The Beatles, reggae, and Duke Ellington. The performance is highly structured and symmetrical, stressing solo performance. Tunes have beginnings, verses and choruses, and formal endings. Singing is done in three-part harmony or solo. In its threefold structure, its stress on individual performance, and its mechanical form, bluegrass music is similar to a Georgian house plan or a matched set of dishes. Even the listeners to this music are engaged in an individual act, in comparison with those who danced together to the tunes played by the old string band.

In those areas where the older musical form was indigenous, bluegrass music often assumes a significantly different form as it is played today. Davidson and Newman remark that bluegrass bands of southwestern Virginia and West Virginia play more in unison and play more tunes from the traditional repertoire, in marked contrast to commercial bluegrass bands, which play almost all Nashville products.[5] True, double stopping is no longer a feature of the fiddle music, and the banjo is played in the new, three-finger style, but the flavor of the music played, and its structure, suggest a blend of old and new very reminiscent of hybrid houses and gravestones; all three seem to be the result of the new tradition glossing over the old, but with the old still lying beneath the surface.

Some argue that a-priori formulations of the sort we are using here to explain the data from the material culture of early America are self-fulfilling, that in one way or another facts are subtly or overtly manipulated to suit the scheme proposed. There is a measure of truth in this. Yet something does seem to have happened to our worldview since 1607, something very basic, which normally resides in our collective unconscious. And contrary evidence is almost non-existent; the facts *do* seem to fit, and comfortably at that. If we can accept this detailing of the changes and the varied evidence for it, we are left with even more basic questions. What brought about the change? Did attitude and perception change our material world, or did the advent of the new, Renaissance-inspired architectural and decorative orders work a change on our worldview?

In his folk housing study, Glassie suggests a number of reasons for the change that are both reasonable and consistent with what we have detailed here: choice of one or another "fashion" is made from a larger range of possibilities, and this factor suggests that the new styles were not only fashionable but comfortably accommodated by a changed view of the world; in time, a social distance grew between individuals, and as the world was perceived as increasingly complex and chaotic, people struggled to maintain control over that part of their world to which they had direct access; identical house facades were a way to maintain a comfortable anonymity combined with stability.

As we see it change over time, other aspects of this dramatic transformation of Americans' worldview become apparent. In the seventeenth century, religion provided a logical and comfortable accounting for a person's place within the world and the universe beyond it, both in life and in the hereafter. The Great Chain of Being, a cornerstone of Elizabethan cosmology, was a structure that in its beautiful simplicity and perfection made every part of the natural world accountable in a hierarchical arrangement. With God at the top, the chain descended through the angels to man, lower animals, and finally to inanimate objects. All was ordered in a way that accounted for a person's position in respect to all of his environment. Predestination, like the Great Chain of Being, was a tenet of all Protestant religions of the seventeenth century. One's place in the hereafter was foreordained at birth, and there was nothing that one could do to alter it. Although there were ways to single out the "elect," those who were destined to eternal glory, no amount of misbehavior would change the predestined course of events, and no amount of exemplary behavior would alter it in the opposite direction. For someone living in America in the seventeenth century, existence and the worldview it produced were so orderly and predictable that the immediate organization of one's surroundings could proceed according to the most practical, the most efficient, and the most responsive solutions to those problems that life presented. Since individual effort and individual status had little effect on the course of life, corporate alliances of various types were the most useful in coping with the world.

All this changed profoundly with the secularization of religion and the scientific revolution of the late seventeenth and eighteenth centuries. The Copernican universe was at the same time humbling and in opposition to the celestial spheres within which the Great Chain of Being was enclosed. Religion became less and less the central, integrating factor of life in a world in which commerce rose dramatically in importance with the opening of the New World. New England, a theocracy before 1650, saw the loss of power by the clergy and its assumption by the merchants as the seventeenth century drew to a close.[6] At this time, the halfway covenant, by which full membership in the Puritan Church could be gained not only by having had directly experienced saving grace but simply by being born of parents who had, signaled a genuine change in the status of God's elect within the Church. The change in the character of New England society from religious to mercantile not only reflects the secularization of life but the new legitimacy of wealth and personal possessions. The medieval guilds, still a strong force in English society at the beginning of the seventeenth century, while protecting the arti-

in small things forgotten

san and assuring a measure of quality control, were corporate. They locked the artisan into a fixed social niche. Their rapid breakdown must in part have been a result of the rising importance of individuals who found a more promising way of life in the new, free-enterprise mercantile system. And only under such conditions would people be in a position to accumulate the material possessions that attested to their status in life.

By the opening of the eighteenth century, the structure that has given comfort and support to the society had collapsed, and in its place people saw only a world becoming increasingly complex and beyond their immediate control. It was at this point that the critical compensations were made that can be seen in the material universe of the time, with balance and order—turning on the individual—assuming paramount importance. Even when the process of change was not complete, the artifacts with which people were identified and that signaled their place in the world were changed in their outward aspect at the very least. In its most pervasive form, the new worldview completely transformed the material world. When the house carpenter who remodeled the Mott house looked with satisfaction on his work, when William Rand of Kingston, Massachusetts, purchased "one dozen blue and white china plates," when Ebenezer Soule put chisel to slate and carved his first cherub, and when Wade Ward of Independence, Virginia, first played chords and picked his banjo in a new way, all were responding in an unconscious way to the material needs of a changed world.

The power and depth of the impact of the Renaissance is all around us, but in ways we rarely appreciate. The sense of loss experienced when one of a set of dishes is broken and the pattern is no longer available, the elaborate filing of silver, glassware, and china patterns with stores so that proper wedding gifts may be purchased, the bilaterality of most mantelpiece arrangements, the positioning of the master of ceremonies and contestants at the Miss America Pageant, and the food we consume and its arrangement on the plate—these and countless other aspects of twentieth-century material culture bear witness to how complete and profound the effect has been. Yet there have been Americans whose cultural heritage has had the strength and integrity to resist the full impact of this transformation, and we must take their story into account, since it gives us another perspective on the American experience.

parting ways

Cato Howe is not a name we will find in our history books. He fought at the Battle of Bunker Hill beside the other troops commanded by Colonel Prescott, but since he was but one of a large army, he shares his anonymity with all the other foot soldiers who have served their country's cause in countless battles from Lexington to Danang. Like them, he returned home after his release from the Army and lived out his life in a modest way. But Cato was different from most of his contemporaries both in the military and at home in Plymouth, Massachusetts.

Cato Howe was black.

If archaeology is a vital contributor to our understanding of all of America's common folk, and what their life meant to them, it is doubly so in the case of our understanding of the black experience in America. Prior to the various emancipation actions, beginning in Massachusetts in 1783 and continuing into the nineteenth century, blacks were chattels, property to be disposed of in any way their owners saw fit. People who held such a status could hardly be expected to have recorded a history of their own in any conventional way, although the strength of oral tradition has preserved more than we might hope. Piecing together black history on a local level is a fascinating and often frustrating process of assembling fragments to form a coherent whole. To gain a true understanding of the story of a people, it is best to detail a picture of their life within a community and then relate that to the larger world. It is in this process that archaeology can contribute in a significant way.

Our knowledge of Cato Howe and his fellow blacks of Plymouth comes from two sources: Fragmentary written records give us a partial picture, lacking in important details. A complementary body of information has been gained by excavating the site of the tiny community in which Cato Howe lived until his death, in 1824. The site of this community is known today as Parting Ways, named for a fork in the road leading from Plymouth to Plympton in one direction and Carver in the other. At the time of its occupation by at least four black families, it was called New Guinea, a fairly common term used over much of Anglo-America for separate black settlements.

Nothing is known of Cato Howe's early life, before his military service. There are references to a Cato in inventories prior to that date, since slaves were included with other taxable property. But Cato was a common slave name, and it is impossible to determine if any of these individuals was the same person. It is a near certainty that he was a slave prior to the Revolution, and along with the other 572 blacks who served in Massachusetts armies, he was given his freedom in 1778 in return for his service. He enlisted as a private in Colonel John Bailey's regiment, and was discharged in 1783. These facts are provided by his military records. Upon returning to Plymouth, Howe probably found himself in the same straits as his fellow blacks who had been given their freedom. While the state saw to it that these people were free, it did little or nothing to provide for their new needs, and subsistence, employment, and housing were difficult to come by. We know nothing of his activities or whereabouts until 1792. In that year, on March 12, the town of Plymouth "voted and granted a strip of land about twenty rods wide and about a mile and a half long on the easterly side of the sheep pasture, to such persons as will clear the same in the term of three years." "Such person" was Cato Howe, and joined by three others—Prince Goodwin, Plato Turner, and Quamany—they established a tiny community on the property. Howe lived out his life on the property. He and the other three men are buried there, where their graves can be seen today, marked by simple field stones. His life at Parting Ways seems to have been a difficult one. In 1818 he applied to the government for a pension, based on reduced circumstances. The pension was granted, and in 1820 he apparently was asked to prove that he had not purposely reduced his circumstances to qualify for the support. His personal property at that time was listed as follows:

Real Estate: None.

Personal Property: 1 cow, 1 pig, 5 chairs, 1 table,
2 kettles, 3 knives and forks,
3 plates, 2 bowls, ax, hoe.

Total Value: 27 dollars.

He stated his occupation as farmer in his deposition. If so, wresting a living from the land where he lived was a taxing job. Today, over a century later, the soil on this tract of land is gravelly and singularly unfertile. To complicate matters even further, he was troubled with rheumatism, and his bedridden wife, Althea, was seventy years old and unable to feed herself. Both had been given assistance by the town before he received his federal pension. Although it is not recorded, Althea Howe must have died shortly thereafter, since Cato married Lucy Prettison of Plymouth in 1821. Three years later, he died, and his estate was probated. His inventory has survived, and attests to his most modest circumstances, as follows:

1 Fire Shovel 8¢ 1 Table 20¢ 1 Table
10¢ 3 Chests $2.12½   2.50½
4 Chairs $1 Bed, Bedstead and
bedding $5.80   6.80
1 Spinning Wheel 25¢ 1 pr.
Handirons 50¢ 1 Iron Kettle 50¢   1.25
1 Iron Pot $1 1 Dish Kettle 20¢
1 Tea Kettle 30¢ 1 Spider 20¢   1.70

in small things forgotten

2 Lamps 12½¢ Tin Ware 25¢ Wooden Ware 25¢ 6 Junk Bottles 30¢	.92½
1 Coffee Mill 12½¢ 1 Mortar 12½¢ Knives, forks, spoons 17¢	.42
1 Flat Iron 20¢ 1 Skillet 15¢ Family pictures 12½¢	.47½
1 Ax 50¢ Crockery and Glass Ware in cupboard $4 Wash Tub 25¢	4.75
1 Rooster Cock 20¢ 4 Hens 80¢	1.00
1 Dwelling House $15 1 Barn $15 1 Cow $12	42.00
	61.82½

After Cato's death, his wife remarried and moved to Boston.

Were it not for Howe's having served in the Continental Army, we would know hardly a thing about him. Except for his inventory and the town's granting him permission to settle on their land, all our knowledge of him comes from military-related records. Even less is known about the three men who were his neighbors in the little community of New Guinea. Had they not also been in the Army, we would know less still. Quamany enlisted at age seventeen and was discharged in 1783. Like Cato, he applied for a pension. Denied it in 1818, he finally received it in 1820, when his guardian, Nathan Hayward, stated that he was incapable of taking an oath, that he was without property, and that he, his wife Ellen, and their two sons were supported by the town of Plymouth. His occupation was listed as laborer. Quamany received his pension of eight dollars monthly. He died in 1833.

Prince Goodwin is the only one of the four whose life before the war is indicated in any way. He was a slave, owned first by Dr. William Thomas and then by his son, Judge Joshua Thomas. He spent only three months in the military and, deserting in 1777, did not receive his freedom, as did the others in 1778. He apparently returned to the Thomas household, since he stayed on as a servant to the judge's widow, and apparently divided his time between New Guinea and the Thomas household. He was married and the father of five children, but there is no record of his death.

Like Howe and Quamany, Plato Turner served in the Army until 1783 and applied for a pension in 1818. We learn little else about him from written records, save that his death is listed in the Plymouth church records in 1819. He was survived by his widow, Rachel.

The ninety-four acres of land on which these four men lived were provisionally granted to Cato Howe in 1792, although there is no record of an outright grant of title to him. The four men cleared the property, built houses, and resided there with the town's permission until 1824. By that time, both Howe and Turner had died. The town authorized the sale of the property in that year, referring to it as land "recently held by Cato Howe, deceased" and "formerly occupied by Prince, man of color." A map drawn by the town clerk in 1840 shows each man's parcel as he had cleared it, and located "Quam's house," even though Quamany had been dead for seven years. Even later, the 1857 map of Plymouth places a "Quam" in the same location in 1840 and a J. Turner also residing on the property. Quam is also on the 1879 Plymouth map, and a "Burr" house is shown at Parting Ways. From this cartographic evidence, there seems a strong possibility that although the town authorized the land's sale in 1824 and explicitly stated that it was formerly held by the four men, they and their families were in some way allowed to live there longer. The land was not sold—small wonder, in view of its poor quality—and remains to this day the property of the town.

In 1975 an archaeological investigation of the Parting Ways community was begun. Renewed interest in the tiny community and its inhabitants had been generated by a special town bicentennial committee on black history, and this group's efforts at first were directed at the cemetery. Its location had not been lost over the years, and as a part of the town's bicentennial program, volunteer groups landscaped the area. At the same time, the committee sought and obtained a vote at Plymouth town meeting to set the land aside for memorial purposes, including the area of the Parting Ways settlement. It was in this area that archaeological excavations were carried out.

If we were to rely only on the documentary sources for our knowledge of the life of the four men who lived at Parting Ways, we would have little on which to proceed.

The information summarized above is all we know. For this reason, the archaeological dimension of the study of the community assumes a much greater significance. In some respects, such investigations take on some of the aspects of prehistoric archaeology, since so little is forthcoming from the historical record. After two seasons of excavation, a whole new set of facts about Parting Ways had been obtained, facts that in many ways place a somewhat different perspective on the simple lives of Cato Howe, Plato Turner, Prince Goodwin, and Quamany.

When the site was first visited, the area later shown to have been the main center of occupation was grassy, with an occasional locust tree, in contrast to the scrub pine and oak that covered the remaining original ninety-four acres. There was only one visible feature, a large cellar hole heavily overgrown with brush. Initial excavations were directed at this feature and a slight depression in the ground a short distance away.

The open cellar hole had all of the appearances of having had a house standing over it in the not too distant past. There was a strong likelihood that it marked the location of the house of the last known inhabitant of the site, James Burr. Burr is known to have lived there in 1895, when a sketch of his life was published in the Boston *Globe*. Burr had an interesting life. He was born and educated in Boston. As a servant to a congressman, he lived in Washington and traveled to England. He later returned to Boston, where he worked as a barber, and in 1861 he moved to Plymouth and settled at Parting Ways. His reason for this move was that he desired to live near his ancestor's grave. Plato Turner was James Burr's grandfather.

This information agrees with the location of a Burr

Figure 13. The Turner-Burr House, Parting Ways, Plymouth, Massachusetts

house on the 1879 Plymouth map. Still there in 1895, at the time of the *Globe* article, the house stood until the early years of the twentieth century. In all probability, the cellar hole was of that house, but it was not until two informants came forth with new information that such an association could be proved. In the August heat of 1975, an elderly couple visited the site while digging was in progress. The man was ninety-one years old and remembered walking past the house as a child; this was in the last years of the nineteenth century. When the *Globe* article was written, Burr lived at the site with his widowed cousin Rachael and her three sons. The informant remembered a lady living there known as Rachael Johnson, her proper married name. This piece of oral history established the cellar as that of James Burr. Later, a photograph of the house was found in the archives of the Pilgrim Society in Plymouth. The house has a small central chimney, and with its shingled exterior and six-over-six windows, looks not unlike any simple vernacular house of the nineteenth century (see Figure 13). Archaeology was to demonstrate that the exterior appearance was deceptive and that it differed from its Anglo-American counterparts in a rather dramatic way.

When excavations were completed on the Burr cellar and in the depressed area nearby, a clear and intriguing set of architectural features had been revealed. The site had never been disturbed by cultivation or other earth removal since it was lived on. As a result, both the focus and the visibility of the features were excellent. The Burr house had been built in two stages, separated by perhaps as much as thirty years. The initial construction had taken place long before Burr moved to the site, and in view of the relationship between the two men, it may have been done by Burr's grandfather, Plato Turner. This first, small structure was twelve feet square, as evidenced by perfectly preserved stone footings. These footings stood on an intentionally mounded earth platform. Artifacts in the fill of this feature and in the trenches that held the footings all point to a construction date at the turn of the nineteenth century, with creamware and pearlware fragments providing the most precise dating evidence. These footings immediately abutted the cellar, and the cellar was beneath a second room, producing an overall ground plan of two contiguous rooms, each twelve feet square. However, the cellar was not added to the initial structure until much later, since no early artifacts were found in association with it and the scant pottery sample it produced dates to the later nineteenth century. The most reasonable explanation of this feature is that the first build was made at about the time the land was first occupied by the four men and that, much later, James Burr enlarged it and added a cellar. Whether he lived for a time in the smaller building, or remodeled it upon moving to Plymouth, is unknown. But the evidence for a two-period construction is quite clear and sufficient. The enlarged house is the one seen in the photograph.

Both sections of the footing showed extensive evidence of fire. Melted window glass, heavy charcoal and ash deposits, and large numbers of nails all attest to the house's having burned in place. A second informant, interviewed in 1976, said that he had used the area to pasture cattle and knew it quite well. He stated that the house burned in 1908. On the other hand, yet another informant recalls visiting Rachael's son Jesse, in a house measuring approximately fourteen by twenty feet, "around the time of the First World War." Also, he stated that this house was later moved to Plympton. Is this the same house? It seems unlikely that it is, since the Burr house is known from archaeological evidence to have burned. If it is not the same house, then somewhere in the area, as yet undiscovered, is a feature that is the remains of Jesse's dwelling. Such a seeming conflict is not at all uncommon when dealing with informants, and the discrepancy is mentioned to illustrate that complete agreement among all sources is rare indeed. As we have said, however, such a lack of fit serves as a warning that further attempts must be made to bring all of the information into reasonable concordance.

Test excavations in the shallow depression nearby produced a sample of pottery all dating to the main period of occupation of the site, from circa 1790 through circa 1840. When these excavations were enlarged, the depression was found to be the location of another cellar. When completely exposed, mapped, and measured, it was a rather puzzling feature. Extensive excavations in the area surrounding the cellar failed to produce any evidence of footing trenches, post alignments, or any other sign of the building that had originally stood over it. Like the Burr footings and cellar, this cellar, too, was twelve feet square. An external bulkhead entrance had originally led into it, but, at some later date, that had been walled in. Two of the cellar walls were of dry-laid field stone, and two others had been covered with boards. This second cellar was filled with refuse and stone. The artifacts in this fill suggest an occupation date during the first half of the nineteenth century, essentially in agreement with the historical record.

We have seen previously that the mean ceramic date for the fill of this cellar is not in agreement with either the known period of occupation or with the *terminus post quem* provided by a stoneware jar known to have been made in Taunton, Massachusetts, at the Ingalls Pottery during the 1840s. The explanation for this discrepancy, that the pottery owned by the occupants of the site was acquired second-

in small things forgotten

hand, is most reasonable. A more striking aspect of this pottery is its very high quality. Types such as hand-painted creamware are not often encountered on New England sites representing people of average means. We might guess that not only was the pottery given to the people of Parting Ways by the townspeople of Plymouth, but it was given by the wealthier ones. Might it not be that the ceramics were provided the men by their former masters? After all, ownership of slaves and the more elegant kinds of dishes are both characteristic of the more elite members of a community. The presence of the kind of pottery normally seen as an indicator of high status on a site occupied by pensioners receiving eight dollars a month should serve as a *caveat* to those who would uncritically use such a single piece of evidence to support a point.

It was while this cellar was being excavated that a discovery was made that raised a number of important questions about the site and its inhabitants. Broken on the cellar floor were two large earthenware jars unlike any before encountered on a New England historical site. Eighteen inches tall, of red, unglazed, well-fired clay, their shape and physical characteristics immediately set them apart from the entire Anglo-American ceramic tradition. These jars were made in the West Indies, and served as sugar containers for shipment to various colonial ports. They are also said to have been used at times for storing and shipping tamarind, a West African cultivated fruit that was grown in the West Indies. By a striking coincidence, during the same season as the Parting Ways dig and again a year later, similar vessels came to light. At least four were found in a contemporary trash pit in Salem, Massachusetts, and one came from a site in Portsmouth, New Hampshire. Their initial discovery at Parting Ways suggests that they might well relate to the African and West Indian background of the people who lived there. In the New Hampshire case, there were blacks living in the household represented by the site. And of course Salem was an important port town in the nineteenth century, dealing in a wide range of West Indian commodities.

How the Parting Ways people came by these jars will never be known; they may have possessed them before moving onto the property or received them, with or without contents, later. But their discovery raised an important issue that bears on any African American site and its interpretation: What degree of African cultural survival can be detected and described when dealing with the material remains of African Americans at an earlier time in the country's history? It would be the height of ethnocentric arrogance to assume that people recently a part of a very different culture would, upon coming to America, immediately adopt an Anglo-American set of values, of ways of doing things, and of organizing their existence. The misleading factor in this case is that the materials with which they were forced to work were the same, for the most part, as those available to the dominant culture which surrounded them. Again we see a strong parallel with language, in this case one that draws on comparable data. In the West Indies, blacks speak hybrid languages known as

Creole languages. Haitian Creole incorporates a French vocabulary, while Dominican Creole employs a modified English vocabulary. But the two share not lexicon but grammar, which in both instances is West African. The same rules are used to assemble the words of two Indo-European languages. Similarly, an Anglo-American set of rules for folk house building can govern the combination of a diverse set of stylistic elements. So it is that while the artifacts available to the members of the Parting Ways settlement were of necessity almost entirely Anglo-American, the rules by which they were put to use in functional combinations might have been more African American. With this possibility in mind, we can look at the material dug from the ground at Parting Ways in a new and potentially more useful way.

In addition to the Burr house and the separate cellar, a third architectural feature was unearthed. Near the second cellar, another depression indicated the remains of some earlier structure. Upon excavation, it was found to be a rectangular pit, roughly eighteen inches deep, measuring twelve feet by nine. Postholes were evident at two of the four corners and at the midpoint of each long side. On the dirt floor were traces of mud walling. The structure that had stood there may not have been a dwelling house, but it seems to have been fairly substantial. Mud-wall-and-post construction is reminiscent of West African building methods, although it did occur in the Anglo-American tradition at an earlier time.

The architecture at Parting Ways provides us with the

first suggestion that an African American mind-set was at work. One measurement runs through all of the excavated structural remains, that of a basic twelve-foot dimension. We have seen that sixteen feet is the Anglo-American standard. At this site, a twelve-foot unit appears to have been used in the same fashion. The Burr house is made up of two twelve-foot modules. The second cellar may actually be the entire footings for a small structure identical to the first build at the Burr house. However, to suggest the use of tiny, twelve-foot-square dwelling houses at Parting Ways in its early occupation, raises the question of a heat source, since no archaeological evidence of fireplaces was found. Yet, even though the photograph of the Burr house shows a small chimney projecting from the roof, there was neither evidence nor space for a hearth and chimney of the sort seen in American houses of the period. Lacking such evidence, it is difficult to determine how the chimney was supported and what general sort of stove or fireplace was employed. But the negative evidence is strong, so there had to be some accommodation for one within the building.

We might suggest that the difference between twelve and sixteen feet is slight, within the range of normal variation. To be sure, there are Anglo-American houses even smaller than twelve feet in one direction, as witness the John Alden foundation of 1630. However, this latter building was quite long, so that the amount of square footage available is almost identical to that observed in the twenty-foot-square Allerton foundation plan. The difference in square footage in a twelve-foot square as opposed to a sixteen-foot square is appreciable, 144 in one case and 256 in the other. This is critical if we are thinking of space in terms of the proxemic relationship between it and its occupants. Yet, if it could be shown that the twelve-foot unit is more broadly characteristic of African American building, a much stronger case could be made. Happily, such a relationship can be clearly demonstrated.

In an article on the shotgun house, John Vlach compares these houses in the American South with those of Haiti, and both with West African house types.[1] The shotgun house is acknowledged as a true African American architectural form. Not only does the Burr house plan conform to the ground plans of shotgun houses, the dimensions are remarkably similar. Beyond this, there are differences. Shotgun houses have end doorways and distinctive windows, while the photograph of the Burr house shows a rather typical New England exterior. Again we see a case of using the material available but arranging it in a way that subtly and more deeply reflects the maker's cultural roots. Sibyl Moholy-Nagy calls the shotgun house an architecture of defiance, in that it is a case of blacks stating their heritage through their building tradition in the face of the dominant culture.[2] The little houses at Parting Ways were probably no less, yet because of the poverty of their builders and the scarcity of material, perhaps the statement was not as blatantly made.

Other aspects of the Parting Ways community show the same differences, albeit not as clearly as the building forms. The settlement pattern, in which all four men appear to have placed their dwellings in the center of the ninety-four acres, might be a significant difference from their Yankee contemporaries. While it may be that they formed a close community simply for mutual reassurance, it is equally likely that the placement of the houses reflects a more corporate spirit than four Anglo-Americans might show in similar circumstances. At the time of the community's formation, the usual pattern of Anglo-American house placement was a scattered one, each family on its own property. Although the town clerk's map explicitly designates discrete portions of the ninety-four acres as having been cleared by each of the four men, they still placed their houses close to one another. Burr's house was probably Plato Turner's. The other cellar has not been clearly identified with any of the four, yet we know that Quamany's house stood just across the road. Since Goodwin spent only a part of his time in the settlement, there is a good chance that the other cellar was Cato Howe's originally. However, he died in 1824 and the cellar was not filled until 1850, presumably at the time the house was either razed or moved. Both archaeological and documentary evidence indicate a continued occupation, perhaps uninterrupted until the twentieth century. But throughout that time, occupation seems to have been concentrated in a small area on the ninety-four-acre tract.

Another striking difference from contemporary Anglo-American sites is seen in the food remains recovered from the Parting Ways site. We have seen that sawing of bone, as opposed to chopping it, appears sometime in the

in small things forgotten

later eighteenth century. No sawed bone was recovered from the site, although one would normally expect all of it to be so cut. It may be the poverty in which the inhabitants lived that is shown by the large number of cow's feet, which make up the majority of the animal bone found. Such parts were of little value to Anglo-Americans, although they could be cooked to yield nourishment. On the other hand, we must not overlook the possibility that these bones might reflect in part a different cuisine, as might the chopped bones from larger cuts of meat. In any case, the animal bone from Parting Ways in no way conforms to that seen on similar sites occupied by Anglo-Americans.

Parting Ways is a very special site, in that it was occupied by at least three families of African Americans who were free of those constraints which might have been imposed on them under the institution of slavery. However marginal they may have seemed to the dominant European community, they were able to organize their world on their own terms from the late eighteenth century onward. Such conditions did not prevail in the Plantation South, where the yoke of slavery was not removed until the time of the Civil War. And while African Americans on all of the plantations coped with the harshness of their condition, they did so in different and often covert ways. It is perhaps due to this difference that the Parting Ways residents left us with a subtle yet clear material statement of their way of organizing their lives. Each constituent element of the archaeological record from Parting Ways, taken alone, is not totally convincing, although powerfully suggestive. But taken as a group, as an expression of African American culture as it was to be seen in early-nineteenth-century Massachusetts, they are indeed compelling, an expression of a worldview not only different from that of the dominant European American culture, but coherent in its own right, attributable to the African heritage shared by Cato, Plato, Quamany, and their families.

Prior to the excavations at Parting Ways in 1975 and 1976, the site was known only as the location of a tiny cemetery which was said to mark the graves of at least some of the inhabitants. A sign at the side of the road informs the reader that:

HERE LIE THE GRAVES OF FOUR NEGRO SLAVES

QUAMANY   PRINCE
PLATO   CATO

THESE MEN FOUGHT IN THE REVOLUTIONARY WAR
AND WERE FREED AT ITS CLOSE.
*The cemetery is located in the original 94 acre plot of
land which was deeded to them by the government when
they were given their freedom.*

The few markers in the cemetery are but the broken stumps of what had been modest green slate gravestones, their inscriptions and designs long since vanished. A discovery made in 1978 not only calls into question the identity of the occupants of the graves, but adds yet one more dimension to the nature of the cultural heritage of the Parting Ways residents, in this case a somewhat enigmatic but dramatic one.

As part of a more extensive survey of the original ninety-four acres for National Register nomination, a large area paved with fieldstone was discovered, just across the road from the original settlement.[3] As is customary with such surveys, excavation at that location was very limited, involving a single test trench fifteen feet long and two and a half feet wide. But excavations were not required to determine the nature of the feature; it was only necessary to remove the thin layer of leaves which had covered it over the years. What came to light was an area some twenty-five by forty-five feet in extent, covered evenly with closely packed cobbles. The southern and western edges of the paving were not sharply defined, but the eastern edge was much more distinct. The northern edge had been obliterated by the widening of the road in 1950. Almost seven thousand artifacts were found atop the paving, and for the most part were concentrated in two discrete areas. The vast majority of these artifacts were fragments of pottery, but there were pieces of shattered glassware as well. All had been intentionally broken on the spot, and as a result most could be partially or fully reconstructed. The pattern that emerged was one that called for comparisons with that associated with African American ritual practices and their West African roots. The two concentrations differed from each other. The more northerly one consisted of two sugar jars, a stoneware jug, miscellaneous pressed glass objects, and a variety of bottles. One of the sugar jars had a hole broken through the base. The second concentration consisted of English white earthenware and a few glass objects. Both concentrations produced a *terminus post quem* in the 1840s. Except for a few pieces of window glass, two nails, and two bricks, no architectural materials were found, and bone or shell was also lacking. Clearly, these concentrations were not the result of domestic trash disposal, nor was the paving in any way the remains of a building of any kind. This negative evidence, combined with the fact that the objects were broken in place, all points to both an intentional construction of the paved area and the placing and breaking of ceramic and glass objects on it in two discrete areas. Such a pattern has a striking parallel to grave decoration practices as they are known from the American South.

Throughout this area, African American graves are ornamented in a distinctive fashion. In *Go Down, Moses,* William Faulkner perhaps summed this up most succinctly:

> . . . the grave, save for its rawness, resembled any
> other marked off without order about the barren
> plot by shards of pottery and broken bottles and
> old brick and other objects insignificant to sight
> but actually of a profound meaning and fatal to
> touch, which no white man could have read.[4]

John Vlach tells us that there is a clear pattern in the types of objects used by African Americans to decorate graves.[5] Bottles and jars predominate, sometimes broken in such a way that they appear to be whole. This was often accomplished by breaking a hole in the bottom, invisible when the object is set upright on the grave. Such breakage could be seen to be done to prevent theft, but Vlach cites extensive evidence that such is not the case, since the community will not disturb grave offerings, even coins, as a result of customs which had their origin in the African past. Similar grave ornamentation is known from all of West and Central Africa, where, as in America, graves and their decorations are seen as inviolate, not to be stolen from. Two themes seem to unite the American and African practices, white objects and objects associated with water. A widespread African system of belief holds not only that the spirits of the dead are white beings, but they reside beneath the water. The connections between African and Southern African American grave decoration are clear and explicit. The extent to which both are related to the paved area at Parting Ways is only slightly less so. True, it is not known whether they mark the location of burials, although it seems very likely that they do. John Vlach, who visited the site in the fall of 1978, commented that whether they marked graves or not, they bore a very strong resemblance to the ritual compounds of the Akan of Ghana. Furthermore, they force us to question the identity of those individuals buried beneath the stumps of green slate gravestones in the cemetery always traditionally identified with the Parting Ways settlement. Given the dates of death of the occupants of Parting Ways, it is most unlikely that their gravestones would have been made of slate, marble having long since replaced slate as the universal material for grave-stones. Furthermore, the cemetery at Plympton, a few miles away, has one eighteenth-century cenotaph commemorating people who had died of smallpox and been buried elsewhere. Several small groups of green slate stones, three or four in number, are to be found in the woods around Plympton, marking the graves of smallpox victims, and it seems very likely that the Parting Ways cemetery is but one more of these.

Of course the Parting Ways site does not reflect the changes we have suggested for Anglo-American culture change, nor should it. Yet in its not fitting this pattern, it reinforces it, since it serves to draw a line beyond which explanation cannot and should not proceed. It tells us that such patterns are applicable only to the remains of a single cultural tradition, and once outside that tradition, other rules apply. During the digging of the Parting Ways site, this difference was brought home again and again when certain implicit assumptions based on our experience in Anglo-American sites did not work out. A large amount of dirt was moved in the name of solving this and that problem formulated from prior experience, and nothing came to light. The occupants of the site constructed their houses differently, disposed of their trash differently, arranged their community differently. But because the artifacts themselves were so familiar to us, the essential differences were disguised behind them, and only when a more basic consideration of different perceptions of the world was made did the picture come into focus.

African American archaeology has become an important and vital component of historical archaeology in the United States. Since the artifactual and architectural remains of these communities are a better index of the life of African Americans in their own terms, they hold great promise of supplementing American black history in a different and important way. Cato Howe, Plato Turner, Quamany, and Prince Goodwin seem like simple folk living in abject poverty when we learn of them from the documents. The archaeology tells us that in spite of their lowly station in life, they were the bearers of a lifestyle, distinctly their own, neither recognized nor understood by their chroniclers.

8

the african american past

Frozen in time and embedded in the American landscape is the track of our collective existence, material culture. It holds the promise of being more democratic and less self-conscious in its creation than any other body of historical material. Although relatively few people wrote in early America, and what was written captured the personal biases of the recorder, in theory almost every person who lived in America left behind some trace of their passing. Perhaps a personal possession, now broken and buried, or a slave cabin in the forest covered with Virginia creeper, or a gravestone tilted by time but still speaking to us across the centuries, or something as humble as the remains of a meal consumed and forgotten—it is all there, and we must not disregard it. If material culture makes a vital contribution to our understanding of the American experience, then it assumes critical importance in the accounting of the African American past. As we have seen, a proper understanding of the residents of nineteenth-century Parting Ways could not have been reached in the absence of the material record, both there and from other places. Such is the case at site after site along the entire eastern seaboard, from New England to Georgia. African American archaeology, accompanied by a large body of scholarship on African American material culture, holds the promise of bringing people who had been marginalized in the writings of their contemporaries back into the picture. As the social satirist Dick Gregory said on a visit to the Parting Ways excavations, "Now we will get a piece of the ink."

In recent years African American archaeology has assumed increasing importance, taking a central place in American historical archaeology. The story that has emerged from the results of excavating sites occupied by blacks, both enslaved and free, from measuring and drawing the plans of hundreds of old houses, and from comparing the results with each other and with various aspects of West African culture, gives us a fresh perspective on the entire American experience. More and more it becomes clear that far from a simple matter of acculturation of Africans to the dominant Anglo-American lifeways, a complex mixing and reformulation of components of both cultures took place, particularly in the American South. Such a process is known as creolization, the interaction between two or more cultures to produce an integrated mix which is different from its antecedents. Few people when viewing the memorable scene in *Deliverance* realize that the young boy playing *Dueling Banjos* is using an African musical instrument while seated on a porch which owes its origins to West African architectural forms. As Mechal Sobel says in her book *The World They Made Together:*

> It was not simply that the politically dominant racial group, the whites, maintained their traditions and imposed them on the blacks. On the contrary, the social-cultural interplay was such that both blacks and whites were crucially influenced by the traditions of the "other." As a result, a new culture emerged in the American South that was a mix of both African and English values.[1]

Sobel sees this process as permeating all of eighteenth-century Virginia society, including "attitudes toward time, understandings of causality and purpose, perceptions of death and the afterlife" and most relevant to our concern, "attitudes toward space and the natural world, as they affected settlement and building."[2] Studies of African American material culture and archaeology have been carried out from Massachusetts to Florida, and as far west as California, but in two areas, the Chesapeake and coastal South Carolina, research has been particularly intensive, and it is on these two regions that we focus our attention. Three aspects of early African American life will be explored: housing, foodways, and ceramics, including a local clay smoking pipe industry.

The form of African American dwellings has varied, both in time and space, as a result of various historical and

in small things forgotten

Figure 14. Shotgun house

cultural factors. We begin with the shotgun house, which we briefly encountered as it related to the spatial dimensions of the Turner-Burr house at Parting Ways (see Figure 14). The shotgun house is the most explicitly African vernacular architectural form to be found in America, showing clear and unambiguous derivation from West African houses in both plan and dimensions. Its emergence on the American landscape is the end point of a path that leads from West Africa through the West Indies to the port city of New Orleans. John Vlach was the first to make these connections clear, and his research provides the definitive statement on the subject.[3] Shotgun houses differ from their European contemporaries in three important ways. They are sited with the gable end facing the nearest thoroughfare, whether a city street or a country road, while Anglo-American houses almost always are placed with the long axis parallel. While both houses are entered from the street or roadside, the difference in placement means that shotgun houses are entered through the gable end while European-derived houses are entered from the long side, either through a central passage or into a hall. The room arrangement of shotgun houses is very different from both hall and parlor and central hall houses; each room leads into another from front to back, with three or more rooms lined up one behind the other. Doors between rooms are usually placed in such a way that one can pass in a relatively straight line from the front entrance to the room farthest to the rear. Indeed, this room arrangement has been said to be the reason for the name "shotgun"; one could fire a gun from one end of the house to the other through the aligned doors. This explanation seems rather far-fetched, and John Vlach has shown that a more likely possibility for the name's origin lies in the Yoruba word for house, *to-gun,* meaning place of assembly. Shotgun houses have rather deep porches on their fronts, which in effect form another room of sorts, an intermediate space linking the outside world with that within. We have already seen that the

in small things forgotten

normal size of rooms of shotgun houses is significantly smaller than the size of rooms of an Anglo-American vernacular dwelling. In room size and arrangement, it is clear that the shotgun house reflects a very different proxemic order, one of closer social interaction, which Vlach refers to as "an architecture of intimacy."[4]

The clarity of the African derivation of the shotgun house is the result of the manner in which it was introduced into the American South. Shotgun houses make their first appearance in New Orleans during the first decades of the nineteenth century. New Orleans' sizable community of free blacks was substantially increased by the arrival of over two thousand free people of color in 1810, most of them from Haiti. The urban Haiti shotgun house is virtually identical to those first built in New Orleans. Both share identical floor plans, placement in relationship to the street, and porches in front. Both the porch and front entrance, Vlach suggests, were derived from the indigenous Arawak Indian house, making the Haitian shotgun house a creolized form, incorporating these features with French building techniques and a floor plan derived from the basic Yoruba two-room house.[5] From New Orleans, the shotgun house spread across the country, changing but little, to be found along all of the major railroad routes, northward along the Mississippi, and even penetrating the coalfields of West Virginia. Wherever we find the shotgun house, its presence is clear evidence of the strength of the African tradition in African American material culture. In the absence of the constraints imposed under a system of slavery, this architectural expression was able to flourish, providing us with the clearest vision of the maintenance of an African architectural tradition in the New World.

In the Chesapeake and in South Carolina, dwellings of African Americans take a different form, both from the shotgun house and from those of each respective region. Along the eastern seaboard, African Americans were not free to construct dwellings that might show clear connections to prior African forms. It is very likely that although slaves actually built the houses in which they would live, there was some measure of control exercised by their owners over just what form their houses would take. Nonetheless, we can see that slave dwellings were not purely European-type structures. Although not as clearly African-derived as are shotgun houses, slave houses in the South are best seen as the product of creolization, in this case between Anglo-American and African house types. In his book *Uncommon Ground,* Leland Ferguson summarizes the findings of archaeologists working on a number of plantation sites in South Carolina.[6] Although the evidence is somewhat ambiguous, a pattern can be seen suggesting a house type quite different from what one might expect had the builders been of Anglo-American stock. Shallow trenches mark the locations of walls in the earlier examples, dating to the mid eighteenth century. Posts along the trenches either served to support clay walls or, alternatively, held woven branches over which clay would have been applied, the traditional "wattle and daub" type of wall known both in England and West Africa. Little evidence of chimneys was

in small things forgotten

present, although one structure had an interior hearth. This lack of chimneys led Ferguson to suggest that most cooking was done outdoors, typical of West Africa, yet there must have been some source of heat, for winters in South Carolina can be quite cold. Room sizes found in one- and two-room houses are close to the norm shown by both shotgun houses and West African dwellings. Later in the century, trenches are no longer present, and post holes—not the massive ones associated with earthfast building in Virginia—have been interpreted as the supports for wattle. These later houses also show evidence of having had chimneys, probably of stick and clay, similar to those found on Virginia sites, and known from photographs of both slave cabins and the houses of poorer white farmers. Room sizes of these later houses are slightly larger. What appears to have been happening in South Carolina was that over time, slave houses became more European in flavor, although at no point did they become identical to the smallest of Anglo-American vernacular houses.

On the basis of presently available archaeological evidence, it appears that in Virginia, earthfast construction was used in building dwellings for slaves. William Kelso has excavated a number of slave houses at Kingsmill, near Williamsburg.[7] While these houses resemble other earthfast buildings of the eighteenth century, there are notable differences. Three houses appear to have had porches, in one case, on all four sides of the building. We shall see that porches are probably of African origin, making their appearance in Virginia in the nineteenth century on the houses of all of Virginia's inhabitants. Their presence on eighteenth-century slave houses at Kingsmill lends a certain weight to this proposition. Another feature that sets apart the Kingsmill slave houses from those of their Anglo-American contemporaries is the presence of numerous small root cellars beneath the floors. Such root cellars have been found on other slave quarter sites in Virginia, including those on Mulberry Row at Jefferson's Monticello. Often called "hidey-holes," these little cellars have come to be taken as a marker of African American ethnicity, although in the absence of a documented African American presence on any given site, such a relationship must remain somewhat speculative for the moment. With one possible exception, the Kingsmill foundations showed no evidence of chimneys. While this may be evidence of outdoor cooking, as Leland Ferguson has suggested, as in South Carolina, there had to have been some source of heat during oftentimes frigid winters. William Kelso has shown that stick and clay chimneys were attached to the house in such a way that they could be pulled away from the house in the event of fire. He based this conclusion on patterns of nail concentrations beyond the end of the slave house excavated at Monticello, and on surviving photographs showing such chimneys leaning slightly away from the house and supported by poles. He went so far as to build such a house, set it afire, and knock away the poles. Captured on film by the BBC, this piece of experimental archaeology showed dramatically that such an arrangement actually worked, the chimney falling away from the house, engulfed in flame,

in small things forgotten

leaving the building unharmed. If stick and clay stacks were the rule in eighteenth-century slave cabins, both in South Carolina and Virginia, one would not expect to find any trace of such a chimney, for were it constructed around posts set into the ground, it would have been impossible to knock it away from the house in the brief time that would be necessary. The chimney would not intrude below ground level, and as a result, would leave no trace to be found by the archaeologist.

By the early nineteenth century in Virginia, at least some plantations were constructing more substantial houses for their slaves. At Flowerdew Hundred, a slave cabin dating to the 1830s was excavated. The house had been set on brick piers, raising it above ground level by a foot or so. In a house of this type, the floor would have been of wood, and access to the space below gained either through a trapdoor or by crawling beneath, given enough room. While such an arrangement would certainly reduce dampness and provide healthier living conditions, it may tell us something about social control as employed by the planter. If, as some have suggested, hidey-holes were used to store valuables, perhaps including things not come by in legitimate manner, such could not be used in a covert fashion in a cabin set on piers above the ground. Standing slave cabins in Prince George County show such foundations, and there is ample room both to see and crawl beneath their floors.

When we piece together what we know about shotgun houses, the Turner-Burr house at Parting Ways, and the archaeological evidence from Virginia and South Carolina, a pattern emerges which has implications of a broader nature, suggesting an ordered and logical explanation of the picture of African American dwellings as a whole. While it should come as no surprise, it appears that to the extent European-American influence on house forms was exercised, it was to the same extent houses became less explicitly African in flavor. We have suggested that the inhabitants of Parting Ways, slaves who had been given their freedom and were thus able to express themselves through their material world, did so in such a way that their African heritage surfaced one more time. The ground plan of the Turner-Burr house shows rooms with dimensions close to those of both shotgun houses and earlier slave houses in South Carolina. The layout of the house differs from those of shotgun houses in the placement of the entrance, which we know from a photograph to have been on the long side of the building. This entry location is likely derived from the dominant, non-African architectural tradition of the region, but we must not discount another possibility. A house with two small rooms, entered from the side, is the basic form over much of West Africa. In addition, John Vlach writes:

> The Yoruba architectural repertoire is quite extensive, ranging from common houses to palaces. But despite the variety, all of the buildings are based on a two-room module which measures ten by twenty feet. . . . This two-room house is essential to the Yoruba architectural system, and consequently was

not easily forgotten even under the rigors of slavery.[8]

Whatever the case, the Turner-Burr house more closely resembles a Yoruba two-room side-entrance building than it does either an Anglo-American house or a shotgun house, and this similarity may well be more than coincidental. The main difference is in the construction material, frame on the one hand and mud on the other. The remains of one mud-walled building were uncovered at Parting Ways, the little nine-by-twelve-foot structure near one of the cellars. This feature in turn is reminiscent of earlier slave houses in South Carolina.

Shotgun houses and the Parting Ways architecture stand at one end of a continuum which ranges through the earlier and later slave houses of South Carolina to the earthfast dwellings of the Chesapeake. The primary factor that appears to shape this continuum is the institution of slavery, and how that affected African Americans in each instance. The first Africans to arrive in the colonies were brought to Virginia sometime before the spring of 1619. A census, or muster as it was called, was taken in the colony between March and May of that year, and it lists as "Others not Christians in the service of the English" four Indians and thirty-two Africans. Of the latter, fifteen were adult men and seventeen adult women.[9] Later in the same year, another twenty-odd Africans were brought by a Dutch ship to the colony. A second muster, taken in 1625, shows seven "negroes" residing at Flowerdew Hundred. One of them, a "young child" of an anonymous "negro woman," may well have been the first black child born on English soil in the New World, and was certainly among the first few true African Americans. We are not certain of the status of these first Africans in Virginia. They might have been slaves, but it is somewhat more likely that they held a status more like that of indentured servants. At least some had Christian names, and in the earlier seventeenth century, religion was the predominant criterion by which one would be enslaved; heathens of any color were considered as potential slaves, property whose progeny would also be owned by another. Christians, on the other hand, were not seen as appropriate chattels, whether black or white. As the seventeenth century passed, the opposition between Christian and heathen slowly gave way to that between black and white, and by century's end, race had become the sole determining factor of who would be enslaved and who would not. Slavery based on the color of one's skin did not arrive full-blown on English American soil, but slowly emerged over a considerable period of time. While Virginia's African population was never large until the last years of the seventeenth century, it was nevertheless a constant presence. Dell Upton's study of changing house size makes it very likely that until the 1680s, both black and white in whatever form of servitude often resided in the same houses as their masters. When this residential pattern changed, it did so as a result of deteriorating social relationships between masters and servants, the majority of whom were English. The first separate residences for servants almost certainly housed more whites than blacks, and in view of the small African population, these buildings were probably constructed largely by European Americans, using an earthfast technology brought from England. It was only as the seventeenth century drew to a close that the balance shifted to a majority of Africans, now fully enslaved, and living apart from their masters. It would only be after this time that the distinctive features of eighteenth-century slave houses that we see at Kingsmill appeared, sub-floor root cellars and porches, added to an architectural form which owed more to its English antecedents. So it is that a combination of an earlier close social relationship between Africans and English and the development of separate housing for servants as well as slaves later in the century led to a house form more outwardly English than that seen in South Carolina, Louisiana, or at Parting Ways in Massachusetts. The Africanisms of Chesapeake slave houses are additions to a pre-existing house type—root cellars and porches—rather than a more creolized blending of elements.

South Carolina had a very different pattern of settlement by Africans than did Virginia. Established at about the time that slave imports increased dramatically, it never witnessed a small black population as did Virginia during the earlier seventeenth century. Africans came into the colony in large numbers from the start, for most of South Carolina's first settlers came from Barbados, not from England, bringing their slaves with them. As the slave trade increased, with more and more Africans arriving in the slave market at Charleston, a separate residential quarter for slaves was already firmly in place, so that opportunities for the kind of close interaction which we see in earlier Virginia were not present. Such separation furnished an environment in which various African cultural traditions could survive and flourish. Furthermore, from the early eighteenth century, South Carolina had a black majority, which remained until the earlier years of the twentieth century. It is in South Carolina and Georgia where we see the strongest retention of a wide variety of African cultural elements. These include the coiled basketry made on the Sea Islands, the Gullah language, a creole using a modified English vocabulary set in a grammatical context more West African in form, a strong woodworking tradition, and African methods of grave decoration. To this we can add housing, as archaeology has shown. In contrast to Virginia, where the earliest slave quarters were conceived as dwellings for both blacks and whites, slave houses built on the Carolina rice plantations were much closer in form to African antecedents, and changed at a slower rate, approaching their Virginia counterparts, but never becoming so European in either outward appearance or construction techniques.

At least two aspects of West African architecture appear to have been incorporated into the construction and design of Anglo-American buildings. Framing techniques brought from England underwent changes in the new American environment, most of them involving some kind of simplification. But Mechal Sobel suggests that in the Chesapeake, and only there, a truly "radical" and even

in small things forgotten

"revolutionary" transformation took place.[10] According to Dell Upton,

> Whereas traditional Anglo-American frames of the type used in New England employ large timbers tied together by complex joints, southern frames consist of pairs of light walls linked at the top. Relatively small major timbers—about four by eight inches—were set at ten-foot intervals, with the spaces between filled by three-to-four-inch studs. . . . Two long walls constructed in this manner were tilted up, and ceiling joists notched at their undersides were dropped on to hold the walls upright. . . . In the southern frame the parts were relatively unspecialized, and could be cut out and assembled with equal ease.[11]

Upton goes on to say that this framing system, which appears during the early years of the eighteenth century, ultimately spread across the country, and can be found in nineteenth-century buildings as far away as California. In another article, Upton writes of the English form of framing becoming "so distorted as to be unrecognizable"[12] in the Chesapeake. However, if the transformation of the frame of Chesapeake buildings was the result of the adoption of African building techniques, it is less a matter of distortion than of the incorporation of non-English techniques into the local tradition. The type of framing described above is very similar to that found over much of

West Africa, including dimensional sizes used for the various parts and the method of assembly of the structure. The date of the emergence of the new method of framing and assembly was just at the time when the African population in the Chesapeake underwent a dramatic increase, making the African derivation of the southern frame highly probable.

The veranda, or porch, also appears to have its roots in West Africa. Writing about the porch in nineteenth-century America, Henry Glassie says

> . . . it was a living space between the indoors and the outdoors, a room that stretched the length of the facade (for all the world like a veranda in Yorubaland) providing a place to escape from the inferno inside, to rock and watch the action on the road.[13]

John Vlach sees an irony in the way in which African architectural influences are so widespread in Anglo-American building that they become essentially invisible.[14] He sees this as particularly so in the case of the front porch. But it is generally agreed that porches of this kind were never a part of the English architectural repertoire. The porch, such as it was, in English houses and those of earlier Anglo-America was a rather small entrance chamber, a vestibule of sorts. But in the hot humid summers of the Chesapeake, a large exterior porch is most appropriate. One

wonders why porches do not make their appearance earlier;
Vlach quotes Pierce Lewis as saying

> . . . gallons of eighteenth-century Virginia sweat
> were spilled before there was a grudging admission
> that the doors and windows of Georgian London
> provided inadequate ventilation for a Tidewater
> summer . . .[15]

Perhaps "grudging" is the operative word here. A porch
would represent a major alteration in the physical appearance of a building. In this, it differs from framing techniques, which do not alter the outward form of the house.
Then too, since Africans undoubtedly constructed many of
the houses for their Anglo-American residents, they would
naturally use framing techniques with which they had a
long familiarity, but when it came to designing buildings,
this was done by Anglo-Americans, and a certain inertia in
the adoption of a major architectural element is not surprising. We have seen that porches have been found on slave
cabins excavated at Kingsmill, dating to the third quarter
of the eighteenth century. This is the earliest evidence that
we have for porches to date. That they were unknown in
New England on the eve of the American Revolution is
shown by a delightful exchange of correspondence between
a builder and his client.[16] One Henry Pelham was attending to the construction of John Singleton Copley's house in
Boston. On July 14, 1771, Copley wrote Pelham from New
York:

Should I not add Wings I shall add a peazer when I return, which is much practiced here, and is very beautiful and convenient.

Pelham answered:

I dont comprehend what you mean by a peazer. Explain that in your next.

Copley replied:

You say you dont know what I mean by a Peaza. I will tell you than. it is exactly such a thing as the cover over the pump in your Yard, suppose no enclosure for poultry their, and 3 or 4 Posts added to support the front of the Roof, a good floor at bottum, and from post to post a Chinese enclosure about three feet high. these posts are Scantlings of 6 by 4 inches Diameter, the Broad side to the front, with only a little moulding round the top in a neat plain manner. some have Collumns but very few, and the top is generally Plasterd, but I think if the top was sealed with neat plained Boards I should like it as well. these Peazas are so cool in Sumer and in Winter break off the storms so much that I think I should not be able to like an house without. . . .

This exchange of letters tells us two things. Porches were not yet generally used or known in Boston in 1771, but they were already "much practiced" in New York. We can assume that they were also coming into general use from New York southward, and had probably spread from the Chesapeake northward by that date. In any case, by the nineteenth century the porch had become a commonplace part of the American house. It was a place to sit and swing, make ice cream, pick a tune or two, and even store a broken wringer washing machine, and we owe it all to those anonymous people who brought it from West Africa.

Excavations of slave quarters from Virginia to Georgia have provided us with a far more complete picture of slave diet and foodways than if we were to rely on documents alone. For the most part, the written record tells us what foods were issued to plantation slaves by the planter as regular rations. Taken at face value, such lists would suggest a diet of repetitive plainness, but when we include foods that we know were consumed evidenced by the bones of various kinds of wildlife recovered from refuse heaps on slave cabin sites, a very different picture emerges. John Otto's study of a plantation on the Georgia Sea Islands is an excellent example of the role played by archaeology in reconstructing the foodways of slave communities.[17] Cannon's Point Plantation was occupied between 1794 and 1860. Two slave quarters, each occupied by ninety-odd people, were located at some distance from the planter's house, and an overseer's house was sited between them. Otto excavated the houses of the overseer and planter, as well as a single slave house at the northern end of the plantation. Since the three structures were some distance from each other, refuse from each could be attributed to the occupants with a high degree of confidence. As one might expect, the greatest differences were those between the planter's house and the slave cabin, and it is from the material recovered from each that Otto gives us a detailed picture of diet and foodways of slave and planter alike.

The slave house was small, measuring approximately seventeen by twenty feet, and set on piers. A single chimney of tabby brick—a mixture of shell, lime, and sand—was located at one end. At least one of its windows was glazed, and a shutter pintle, door pintle, and lock bolt suggest that there was some modest degree of privacy. Based on the number of slaves on the plantation and the number of houses, we can assume that the building housed between seven and nine people. A refuse area was located some distance to the south of the house. When we combine the information recovered from the refuse area with what we know of the house, we are able to piece together a picture of a world that few if any saw, other than those who were responsible for its construction.

The refuse deposit consisted largely of animal bones and shattered ceramic and glass wares, but also produced lead shot, a percussion cap, and a single English gun flint. Gun parts and shot have been found on other slave sites, and while we can never be certain that they tell us that slaves had access to firearms, the probability is quite high.

in small things forgotten

In view of the remarkable diversity of species represented by the faunal remains, it becomes even more so. No fewer than twenty-two different species of wild animals are represented. Domesticated animal food remains included rabbits, pigs, cattle, sheep, and chickens. But fully 44 percent of the edible meat available to the inhabitants of the house was from wild species, and included opossum, rabbit, raccoon, clapper rail, two species of turtle, and fifteen species of edible fish. This variety of fish and game tells us that the slaves were obtaining these animals from a wide range of habitats—sounds, tidal rivers, marshes, ponds, forests, and grasslands—which would require a significant amount of spare time. We know from the records that Cannon's Point employed a so-called task system in organizing slave labor. Each hand was responsible for cultivating a set number of quarter-acre plots, and once this had been done, the balance of the day could be used, in the words of the planter, "to employ . . . what remains of daylight in their own gardens, in fishing, or in dancing—in short, as they please." This should not be seen as an act of generosity on the planter's part, but rather a means whereby he could economize on slave rations. Rations at Cannon's Point consisted of nine quarts of corn for each adult, and five to eight for children per week. Rice, flour, and molasses were also issued. But for the occasional piece of fresh meat at slaughter time, meat rations were limited to three pounds of salt pork and fish weekly. This amounts to slightly less than a half pound of protein-rich meat each day, hardly an adequate amount to sustain a person who is engaged daily in hard labor. It was clearly in the planter's best interest to keep his workforce healthy, so by permitting and providing time for hunting and fishing, he was able to achieve this with the least amount of investment.

Combining the variety of meat at hand with vegetables from their own garden plots, the slaves seem to have prepared a variety of stews for the most part, for the vast majority of ceramics recovered from the refuse deposit were bowls of one kind or another, with dinner plates being quite scarce. The bones of the larger animals were chopped rather than sawn, reminiscent of both Parting Ways and all Anglo-America at an earlier time. The bowls used by the Cannon's Point slaves for food consumption were largely of a type of pearlware known as annular ware. Annular ware is decorated with a series of concentric colored bands on the exterior of the bowls, placed horizontal and parallel. It was the second least costly of all the pearlware products of the Staffordshire ceramic industry[18] and we often find it on sites associated with people who held a subservient station in life. Not only is it commonly found on slave sites over the entire South, but also in the Indian quarters at Franciscan missions in California and even at a fort occupied by a Cape Colored regiment in nineteenth-century British South Africa. In every case, annular ware appears not to have been of hand-me-down status, but rather to have been acquired by those in control, to be issued at appropriate intervals. John Otto suggests that because of their distinctive type of decoration, "they appealed to a steady group of customers," including black slaves. But this seems very unlikely, and their presence at slave sites seems one more case of the planter's management of available capital. The appearance of annular ware on slave sites of the early nineteenth century may well mark the time when mass-produced English pottery became inexpensive enough to be purchased in quantity for issue to slaves, for as we shall see, another kind of bowl is typical of the eighteenth and late seventeenth century, produced by the slaves themselves.

When we compare the faunal material recovered from the planter's house with that from the slave quarter, significant similarities and differences appear. The planter's household actually consumed a slightly higher amount of fish and game than did those of the slaves. But the species are not entirely the same, with "high-status" game food such as venison and alligator present, as well as marine turtles. Pork was slightly more common than beef in the planter's diet; in the slave faunal remains, both appear in equal amounts. More telling is the parts of cattle and pigs consumed in each case. Whole hindquarters are represented in the planter's refuse, while that of the slaves produced teeth, scapulae, pelves, and forelegs, mostly from poorer cuts of meat. In contrast to the slave faunal material, that from the planter's house shows the bones to have been sawn rather than chopped. A high percentage of transfer printed dinner plates tells us that the planter's pattern of food consumption was typical of that of all of Anglo-America at the time. Yet only a short distance to the south of the planter's house, there were people partaking of a foodways tradition of a very different kind, one that archaeology has shown to stretch back in time to the late seventeenth century, with deep African roots.

As early as the 1930s, a distinctive kind of pottery was turning up on sites in the Chesapeake. Gray to brown in color, it was an unglazed ware, handmade and fired at a relatively low temperature. The commonest shape was a shallow bowl, but other forms were also produced, including skilled copies of European vessels—three-legged pipkins, milk pans, porringers, punch bowls, chamber pots, and even teapots (see Figure 15). It was not until 1962 that its existence was formally recognized; prior to that date, it was simply noted, cataloged, and stored. The archaeologist who called attention to this pottery was Ivor Noël Hume, in a brief article in the *Bulletin* of the Virginia Archaeological Society.[19] He suggested that it had been made by local Indians to trade with the English colonists, since it bore a certain resemblance to the local Native American pottery. Hume gave the name Colono-Indian to the ware, and thought that it had been made on the nearby Pamunky, Chickahominy, and Mattaponi reservations. Three years later, Lewis Binford reported on Colono-Indian ware from surface collections made on five sites in southeastern Virginia, and attributed its manufacture to two local Indian groups, the Weanock and Nottoway. He suggested that the flat bottoms exhibited by the vessels might be seen as evidence of cooking on European-type hearths, since Indian pots have rounded bases better suited to standing in ash and coals. Colono-Indian ware was initially thought to be a

in small things forgotten

Figure 15. Colono ware shapes

strictly local product, found only in the Chesapeake, and until the late 1970s no one thought to ask if the pottery might have been made by another group of people familiar with European cooking methods and who came from a tradition of handmade pottery—African Americans.

It is significant that the first archaeologists to question the identity of the makers of Colono-Indian ware were from the University of South Carolina, and had done extensive fieldwork in that state. By the decade of the seventies, it was abundantly clear that far from being produced only in the Chesapeake, Colono-Indian ware was to be found in every state along the eastern seaboard from Maryland to Georgia, precisely that area where plantation slavery had been established. While Stanley South had raised the possibility that at least some of the Colono-Indian ware from South Carolina was made by Africans, it was Richard Polhemus who stated what now seems obvious, that Africans, not Indians, were its primary if not exclusive makers. In a 1977 report on the Tellico blockhouse, an early-nineteenth-century site in Tennessee, Polhemus wrote:

> The single historically documented factor linking "Colono-Indian" pottery-producing settlements on the coastal plain of Virginia and North Carolina with those in the uplands of South Carolina and the Tellico blockhouse is the presence of Negroes at the sites in question.[20]

He went on to compare the pottery with that from Nigeria and Ghana, and found that the similarity was great. Certain Ghanaian pieces were indistinguishable from South Carolina ones. Both were flat-bottomed, burnished, grit-tempered, and had incised X's on their bases. Leland Ferguson, a colleague of both South and Polhemus, commented in 1980 that

> with this important observation, the lid was cracked on a box that has sat covered with dust in the darkest corner of North American historic sites

in small things forgotten

archaeology, the contribution of Afro-Americans to the pottery that we call Colono-Indian.[21]

Ferguson was the first to propose the term "Colono ware" to designate this pottery, and that usage has since become universal.

Three aspects of Colono ware provide us with a firm basis on which to argue its African American production—its pattern of occurrence over time, its geographical distribution, noted above, and its physical form.[22] In Virginia, the colony where Africans were present from the first quarter of the seventeenth century, Colono ware does not make its appearance until the last twenty-odd years of that century, and becomes increasingly common on sites of the eighteenth century, reaching its highest frequency between 1750 and 1800. During the early years of the nineteenth century, its popularity appears to have declined, and by 1820 it had all but vanished from the scene. In South Carolina, a fortification ditch at Charleston, cut in 1670 and filled in 1680, contained large quantities of Colono ware, which tells us that the pottery appeared fully developed from the first decade of the colony. The Barbadian settlers of South Carolina brought slave potters with them. The colonial pottery industry in Barbados dates to the mid seventeenth century or earlier, and produced both wheel-made wares and handmade forms very similar to American Colono ware. As in Virginia, Colono ware became increasingly common during the eighteenth century, and disappeared during the early years of the nineteenth. When we consider the pattern of population change for the two groups who might have produced Colono ware, a simple but compelling fact emerges. As the native population declined, and the African population burgeoned, Colono ware became increasingly common. Virginia is an excellent case in point. There the native population underwent a dramatic reduction in numbers as the seventeenth century passed. By 1669, the number of Indian males in the colony had dwindled to a mere 279, representing nineteen tribes. Writing of the Virginia groups in 1781, Thomas Jefferson said:

> Chickahominies removed, about the year 1661 to Mattapony River. . . . They retained however their separate name so late as 1705 and were at length blended with the Pamunkies and the Mattaponies and exist at present only under their names. There remain of the Mattaponies three or four men only, and they have more negro than Indian blood in them. They have lost their language, have reduced themselves, by voluntary sale, to about fifty acres of land, which lie on the river of their own name, and have, from time to time, been joining the Pamunkies, from who they are distant but ten miles. The Pamunkies are reduced to about ten or twelve men, tolerably pure from mixture with other colours. The older ones among them preserve their language in a small degree, which are the last vestiges on earth, as far as we

know, of the Powhatan language. . . . Of the
Nottoways, not a male is left. A few women constitute the remains of that tribe.[23]

Jefferson was writing about four of the groups once
thought to have produced Colono ware for trade with the
Europeans; with numbers so small it seems quite unlikely
that such could have been the case. This is especially so
considering that he penned these words at the time when
Colono ware in Virginia appears to have been produced in
very large quantities. Leaving aside for the moment the
question of why Colono ware appears much later than
Africans in the colony, the steady increase in Colono ware
during the eighteenth century matches closely the pattern
of African population growth in Virginia.

We have seen that in South Carolina, Colono ware
was present from the first years of the colony. There, as in
Virginia, its popularity increased through the eighteenth
century, and faded sharply in the early nineteenth. In both
places, its disappearance was probably the result of the
greater availability of inexpensive Staffordshire wares, of
the type which we have seen from the slave refuse at Cannon's Point. While the pattern of occurrence over time of
Colono ware in Virginia and South Carolina is essentially
the same, there are significant differences in the shapes that
were produced, and these further strengthen the argument
that African Americans were the makers of the pottery.
The close copying of European ceramic shapes in Colono
ware seen in Virginia is conspicuously rare in South Caro-

lina. There, the usual shapes found are three, large jars, small jars, and shallow bowls. The most reasonable explanation for this comes from those differences we have seen between African American residential patterns in the two colonies. The relatively small African population in Virginia resided at least in part in the same house as the planter, along with white indentured servants. It was only at the time the slave population began to increase during the last quarter of the seventeenth century that slaves, along with servants, were moved to separate quarters. Under such circumstances, it is logical to assume that during the time African Americans were living in the same house as their white masters, they became familiar not only with European foodways but also with the kinds of ceramic vessels used in preparing and consuming food. But once removed to separate quarters, slaves had to make do without the various items of equipment available to them before in the master's house. Slaves were issued a minimal amount of equipment for their own use, often little more than an axe and an iron pot or two. Under such circumstances, household production of ceramics would almost certainly take place, and in their shapes and use would reflect both European and African foodways. This would account for both the time of appearance of Colono ware in Virginia and the various forms in which it was produced. In South Carolina, there was no opportunity for slaves to gain a close familiarity with European ways of cooking and the vessels used. Separate quarters set at a considerable distance from the planter's house were present from the colony's beginnings, and this pattern continued through the following two centuries, right up to the Civil War. The limited repertoire of shapes of Colono ware vessels is just what we would expect under such circumstances. When we consider these shapes as they relate to African foodways, they can be seen to be a sort of least common denominator of various West African cooking practices. Basic to West African foodways, both now and in the past, was a meal consisting of two parts. Large jars are used to cook one of a number of starchy carbohydrates, such as rice, manioc, or corn. Smaller jars serve as containers in which to stew a mix of vegetables, meats, and various spices. The meal is served by placing the carbohydrate in a shallow bowl, ladling the vegetable and meat mixture over it, and consuming it with the fingers. We need only to think of gumbo, an American dish with clear African roots, including its name, to visualize better what such a meal would be like. Meat such as sausage, chicken, shrimp, or fish is cooked with celery, onions, and peppers in a seasoned sauce and served over a bed of rice. Even okra, the thickening agent for gumbo, is of African origin. In eighteenth-century South Carolina, this foodways pattern survived almost unchanged from what it had been in the African homeland, largely free of the external influences that were present in earlier Virginia.

Certain economic factors may have been at work which would explain the increasing production of Colono ware during the eighteenth century. In his 1962 article, Noël Hume explained the presence of Colono ware on Virginia sites as the result of planters acquiring pottery from the Indians for use by slaves, "being loath to purchase fancy English pottery" for them.[24] But we must ask why it had to be "fancy," given the low price of locally produced coarse earthenwares; these would have sufficed just as well, and the supply would have been more assured. But with large numbers of slaves on many plantations, even inexpensive earthenwares would represent an investment on the planter's part. In the same way that allowing slaves to procure much of their own food was a cost-cutting measure for the planter, permitting and perhaps even encouraging the production of pottery by slaves would have achieved the same result. There would certainly have been a built-in workforce, and the supply would have been constant and ample. With the African population growing at a steady rate, if the dwindling Native American population had been producing the Colono ware, there would have been an increasing demand accompanied by a decreasing supply, far too great a gap to allow for the trading of Colono ware from the Indians to the degree that would have been required to provide for an ever larger number of people.

The evidence for the production of Colono ware by African Americans is compelling, and while not everyone accepts the argument, it is difficult to ignore. Yet one more body of evidence must be considered, for it provides us with a complementary perspective on the whole question of African American craft production in seventeenth-century Virginia, as well as lending even greater credence to the production of Colono ware by slaves. As we have seen, the attempts by the Virginia colony to achieve some measure of economic independence from England during the seventeenth century involved a number of local industries. Among these was the production of clay smoking pipes, similar in shape to those made in England, but made from a tan clay, and often elaborately decorated with a wide variety of designs (see Figure 16). These pipes make their appearance on sites dating after the 1630s, and their production continued through the early years of the eighteenth century. Like Colono ware, they had been found on sites since the 1930s, but little attention was paid to them until 1979 when Susan Henry published a paper on them entitled "Terra-Cotta Tobacco Pipes in 17th Century Maryland and Virginia."[25] Henry's main question had nothing to do with who might have made the pipes, but rather was directed at the relationship between their production and economic changes in the import trade. But she attributed them to the local Indian peoples, and used the term Colono Indian, following Noël Hume's use of the designation. Like him, she suggested that they were made by the local Indians for trade with the European colonists.

Some of these pipes appear to have been made by hand; others show clear evidence of having been made in a mold of the type used in English pipe manufacture. Two methods of decoration were used: stamping, and designs that were produced by rolling some kind of toothed implement through the clay, perhaps a watch cog. These rouletted designs were filled with a white substance, producing a pleasing contrast to the tan clay of both bowls and stems. While stamped designs continued in use through the early eighteenth century, motifs produced by rouletting appear not to have been applied to pipes after circa 1680, at about the same time that Colono ware made its first appearance in Virginia. But if rouletted pipes were made by Indians, why does their production stop when it does, and is it a coincidence that it does just as Colono ware begins to be produced? The answer may lie in the designs themselves, and their possible origin.

Fish, horned animals, stars, ships, and a variety of geometric motifs appear on the pipe bowls, and the stems are frequently decorated in simple designs of lines and triangles. While many of the geometric motifs are so general as to make any stylistic comparison to other decorative traditions difficult, there are certain ones that are not from the repertoire of either Europeans or Indians, but distinctive enough to be recognized as having probable West African derivation. The first person to call attention to this possibility was Matthew Emerson in a 1988 University of California, Berkeley, doctoral dissertation entitled "Decorated Clay Tobacco Pipes from the Chesapeake." In this work, he proposed the alternative adjective "Chesapeake" as a replacement for the older term Colono Indian, or Colono, which some had used following Leland Ferguson's lead. Of the motifs with possible African derivation, the most convincing is the so-called Kwardata, a very individualistic design which is identical in both Chesapeake and West African examples. In Nigeria, the Kwardata design symbolizes the transition from youth to manhood. It is created by defining a connecting band of diamonds with parallel punc-

in small things forgotten

Figure 16. Chesapeake smoking pipes

tate lines which act as a background, the design itself being negatively formed (see Figure 16a). Equally striking is a motif created by several concentric arcs, with a row of circles above them (see Figure 16b). This design is absent from the local Indian repertoire, and has a close West African parallel. The "double bell" motif, two arcs flanking a horizontal line, is found both on Chesapeake pipes and on a smoking pipe from Cameroon (see Figure 16c). There are other designs that while not as convincing as the three mentioned, are nonetheless suggestive. Stars with sets of circles at the ends of their points are not found in the native American decorative tradition, and while stars alone are commonly used in many parts of the world, the use of circles to embellish the end points of various motifs is common in African decorative arts. Four-legged animals are found on some Chesapeake pipes, some with horns (see Figure 16d). These horned animals have been identified by some archaeologists as deer, and one name given to the motif is the "running deer" design. But the animals on the pipes have horns that look far more like those of antelope or goats, pointing backward rather than being erect as are deer antlers. While deer would be the only horned animals known to the Indians of Virginia, Africans would be familiar with both goats and antelopes.

While highly suggestive, all of these motifs are not sufficient evidence to permit the attribution of Chesapeake pipe decoration to African artists. But they do provide a starting point from which to explore further the possible relationships between these pipes and blacks in seventeenth-century Maryland and Virginia. Unlike Colono ware, Chesapeake pipes were in all likelihood made for sale. One senses that they were not made in many locations, but widely traded. Their production required a somewhat more sophisticated technology than that involved in making Colono ware. The molds used in making some of the pipes were either brought from England or manufactured in Virginia. As yet, none have been found, leaving that question unresolved. But whether English or locally made molds were used, the technology involved—shaping the clay, placing it in the mold, and boring the stem with wire—was unknown to both Native Virginians and Africans. White filled rouletted designs are a common feature of a number of West African pottery traditions, but absent from both Native American and European ones. It would seem, then, that Chesapeake pipes are a true creole form, combining at least in part an English technology with decorations done in a manner with close African connections. When we consider the geographical distribution of Chesapeake pipes, it becomes possible to suggest an explanation that accounts for the facts known about them as well as about Colono ware. Unlike Colono ware, which has been found from Virginia to Georgia, Chesapeake pipes have a limited distribution. They come from sites in the Chesapeake east of the fall line, precisely that area where the earliest African population was to be found. This was the region where the African and European population interacted most closely prior to the removal of slaves and servants to separate quarters. Living as well as working together, the two groups would have created an ideal context in which to produce artifacts such as Chesapeake pipes. But when both slaves and servants were removed from the immediate physical world of the planter, a fundamental change in the quality of social intercourse may well have taken place. The decoration of Chesapeake pipes by Africans could have continued under the new arrangement, but it did not. While such pipes were made into the early years of the eighteenth century, these later examples are mostly mold-made, look more like their English counterparts than before, and are decorated by stamping in English fashion. In a way, then, Chesapeake pipes and Colono ware are the same thing, at a higher level of abstraction. They are artifacts produced wholly or in part by Africans, and their complementary distribution over time bears witness to nothing less than the passing of an entire social order. We know less about the nature of black-white social interaction in the earlier seventeenth century than about that of later times. There is a tendency to project the image of plantation slavery made famous by writers such as Alex Haley and Margaret Mitchell in an uncritical fashion on these earlier times, where in fact, a very different kind of community may have existed, closely knit, and one in which servitude rather than the color of one's skin dictated the social order. Such a community would be expectable in a situation where those of lesser social standing were of both European and African origin, and would change only when the demographic balance shifted to the full-blown racially based slavery which appeared as the seventeenth century drew to a close. Historians have suggested that European attitudes toward blacks, whether slaves or servants, were indeed different in the earlier seventeenth century. Edmund Morgan, while admitting the relative scarcity of written information on black-white relationships in Virginia before 1660, writes,

> While racial feelings undoubtedly affected the position of Negroes, there is more than a little evidence that Virginians during these years were

ready to think of Negroes as members or potential members of the community on the same terms as other men and to demand of them the same standards of behavior. Black men and white serving the same master worked, ate and slept together, and together shared in escapades, escapes and punishments.[26]

Morgan goes on to point out that before 1660 some of the blacks, perhaps a majority, were slaves, but others were servants and some were free. They could earn wages and even use the money to purchase their freedom. The historical record for this period is not as strong as we would like, so that any additional piece of information is indeed valuable. The pattern of occurrence of both Colono ware and Chesapeake pipes not only provides archaeological support to Morgan's thesis, but also fits comfortably with what we know about the plantation community at an early time. An older kind of community gave way to a new order, one that was to remain for the most part unchanged until the national ordeal of the Civil War. Archaeology has contributed to our understandings of this transformation, if only in a modest fashion.

African American archaeology will continue to be a major component of the work of historical archaeologists in the years to come. As it does, we will sharpen our approaches to the excavated material, to ensure that we recover the maximum degree of understanding. Much has been written in recent years about "ethnic markers" as they attest to an African American presence on a site. Objects such as pierced coins, cowrie shells, beads—particularly blue ones—and quartz crystals are seen as evidence that African Americans were once in residence. But no quantity of such objects can provide absolute proof of such a presence when taken in isolation, in the absence of independent documentation. And when such a presence is demonstrated in the documents, what is the need for archaeological substantiation? True, they can be seen as "africanisms"—survivals—but given what we know from the broader archaeological record and the work of scholars of African American material culture, this comes as no surprise. A far more productive approach to understanding the archaeological record of African Americans is to work on sites such as Cannon's Point, Parting Ways, or Kingsmill, to name but a few, and attempt to piece together the whole fabric of a way of life, connecting foodways, dwelling houses, community layout, pottery, and smoking pipes into a coherent, logical whole. What has already emerged from the work of archaeologists on the many sites so far investigated is a sense of the creation in the past of a new way of life, one which owes much of its form to the strength of a culture that survived the middle passage and the rigors of life under the oppression of slavery. Archaeology, not the written record, allows us to look into another world, which in its rich and varied form has made a vital contribution to the culture of all Americans as we know it today.

small things forgotten

Samuel Smith, Cato Howe, Nathan Hayward, Jonathan Fairbanks, Isaac Allerton, Miles Standish—all are names we have encountered as we have surveyed the objects left behind by them and so many others, objects that in a special way tell us of our past and their world. Special because, in the telling, we have gained insights that would have been very difficult to obtain were we to rely solely on the written record. Writing, which to modern Americans seems an almost universal skill, tends to mask the differences between ourselves and the Americans of earlier generations. Obviously the literate minority of early America were more like us at least in that one respect, and since the writing is in English, archaic as it sometimes is, we feel a community with the writers of the past that is misplaced when it is extended to everyone who lived. Were we to confront any of the men named above, we would experience a sense of culture shock as profound as if we had encountered a member of any other of the world's exotic cultures. We mistakenly think of Americans in the seventeenth century as ourselves but somehow simpler, "quaint" perhaps, but people with whom we would feel an instant empathy. In fact, the pre-1750 Anglo-American world was assembled according to a different set of rules, as we have seen, and the contrast between then and now is great. Recognizing this fundamental difference permits us to consider the people of that time more in their own terms, rather than in those categories we impose upon them. For example, in many historic-house museums we are shown the "borning room," a special room wherein babies were born, a place to which mothers repaired prior to childbirth and remained some time after. As best we can determine, such a room never existed. What we have learned about space use in seventeenth-century vernacular houses makes such a specialization very unlikely; the word appears in no inventory of the period, nor is it to be found in the Oxford English Dictionary. It is likely a designation coined much later, probably in the nineteenth century, based on the "logical" assumption that according to modern standards of privacy and behavior such a room must have existed. This sort of attribution of function exemplifies an imposed category, based on our own cultural experience underlain by an implicit assumption of great cultural similarity between new and old America. Such "common sense" judgments have led to the unfortunate clean-and-sterile aspect of many of America's outdoor museums. Guides in starched costumes direct the visitor through neatly arranged houses often furnished with matching artifacts that are not typical of the time being revisited, homes that seem to have been inhabited by people who subsisted largely on the herbs growing in the adjacent garden and who dipped enough candles to light a small town. Such an exhibit ignores the cluttered conditions of early houses amply documented in the inventories and the different way of ordering the physical world, as we have observed, and places an undue emphasis on a world flooded with candlelight. It tells us far more about the minds of its contemporary creators than it does about the thoughts and concerns of the people whose life it is meant to represent.

If such a misreading of the past meant only that museum exhibits were too often overly neat, we would have little need for concern. Unfortunately it also reflects our view of the American past as a romantic time when things were prettier, problems fewer, life simpler, and people kindlier disposed toward their fellows. Such was not the case, and when we view ourselves in comparison to such a distorted view of our past, our present situation seems far more desperate than it is. Pollution is not new: water was undrinkable in seventeenth-century English cities, and archaeological excavations on the banks of the Piscataqua River, in New Hampshire, show that there was a higher level of contamination there in the nineteenth century than today. Simple people—the folk we romanticize so and idealize as having had very altruistic human values—in fact were suspicious of outsiders, intolerant of any change that might threaten their well-ordered world, and capable of savage actions. The dark side of peasant life is little appreciated, but it was real and pervasive, as any reader of Jerzy Kosinski's novel *The Painted Bird* knows and will never forget. A true understanding of the very fundamental differences between ourselves and our forebears of two centuries ago is critical if we are to judge our present condition objectively. Such an understanding is greatly abetted by considering the kinds of evidence from which those differences emerge clearly. Archaeological materials comprise such evidence, since they allow us to see into the past not through the writings of people who are communicating their particular view of the world but through human actions that affected the material world in a broad and general way.

When we began our survey of early American artifacts and their place in the life of the people, we saw that the documentary evidence was of great importance. We have now learned that while this is so, the artifactual evidence is more complementary in nature, and depends on and mutually supports the written record. The idea of a changing worldview can even be used to reexamine certain important events in American history from a slightly, but significantly, different viewpoint. Two documents of great importance in American political history, the Mayflower Compact and the Declaration of Independence, show an interesting contrast in the way they acknowledge the individual. The Compact stresses the larger community, and the individual is not considered: "[we] . . . covenant and combine ourselves together in a civil body politic . . . and promise due submission to the general good of the colony." The Declaration, as every school child knows, states: ". . . that all men are created equal, that they are endowed by their Creator with certain unalienable rights, that among these are Life, Liberty, and the pursuit of Happiness. . . ." While this difference in no way requires archaeological evidence to allow its understanding, each was peculiarly suitable to the needs of the people for whom it was written, as evidenced by the patterns shown by their possessions and dwellings. Abolition of slavery, which has its beginnings in America in the late eighteenth century, also might relate in some way to the importance of the individual that was emergent at that time. Only when the conditions of life that slavery imposed were appreciated on an individual basis, a one-to-one understanding, would consciousness and conscience be sensitized to these problems.

In our world today, other lessons gained from thinking about artifacts might be applicable. The little community of Parting Ways was probably seen by its contemporaries as simply a collection of houses occupied by people who for all intents and purposes were little different from them except for their station in life. Yet America was not a melting pot in the eighteenth century, and it is not one today. In their own way, the black settlers of Parting Ways maintained their cultural heritage in the face of adversity. And today people whose history has not been a part of the Anglo-American past hold similar cultural treasures in trust. We are not usually conscious of these other patterns, for our own culture is an awesome presence, but they are there.

As late as 1957, an expression of another order of life was made by a people who to all outward appearances were thoroughly Anglicized. The town of Fort Thompson, South Dakota, was established in the late nineteenth century as the center of the Crow Creek Indian Reservation. Laid out by government agents, it exhibited a grid plan identical to almost every other town in the state. When the construction of the Big Bend Dam, on the Missouri River, was begun, the town had to be moved, since the center axis of the dam was projected immediately over the townsite. The Sioux Indian residents were asked where they would like their houses moved, and with the help of Corps of Engineers heavy equipment, placed them in a long, attenuated line along the second terrace of the river. The houses were relocated in circular sets, which almost certainly reflected the old concept of a community held by the elders in the town, who were most influential in the new arrangement. Each house cluster was a family group, and while the new arrangement was never properly studied or mapped— it was relocated a second time a few years later—there seems no other explanation for the pattern than its being one that the people themselves felt most suited their social needs and that had been theirs before the reservation community was established.

Historians distinguish between primary and secondary sources. Primary sources include first-person accounts, court records, probate materials, and all those documents produced directly by the people who are being studied. Secondary sources are in essence secondhand, one step re-

in small things forgotten

moved from first-person immediacy. Yet even a primary source, having been written by one individual, must reflect that person's interest, biases, and attitudes. To the extent that it does, such a source is secondary to some degree, in inverse proportion to its objectivity. Total objectivity is not to be expected in human judgment, and the best we can do is recognize and account for those subjective biases we carry with us.

Material culture may be the most objective source of information we have concerning America's past. It certainly is the most immediate. When an archaeologist carefully removes the earth from the jumbled artifacts at the bottom of a trash pit, he or she is the first person to confront those objects since they were placed there centuries before. When we stand in the chamber of a seventeenth-century house that has not been restored, we are placing ourselves in the same architectural environment occupied by those who lived there in the past. The arrangement of gravestones in a cemetery and the designs on their tops create a *Gestalt* not of our making but of the community whose dead lie beneath the ground. If we bring to this world, so reflective of the past, a sensitivity to the meaning of the patterns we see in it, the artifact becomes a primary source of great objectivity and subtlety.

It is terribly important that the "small things forgotten" be remembered. For in the seemingly little and insignificant things that accumulate to create a lifetime, the essence of our existence is captured. We must remember these bits and pieces, and we must use them in new and imaginative ways so that a different appreciation for what life is today, and was in the past, can be achieved. The written document has its proper and important place, but there is also a time when we should set aside our perusal of diaries, court records, and inventories, and listen to another voice.

Don't read what we have written; look at what we have done.

in small things forgotten

notes

1
RECALLING THINGS FORGOTTEN

1. Jack Larkin, *The Reshaping of Everyday Life 1790–1840* (New York: Harper & Row, 1988), p. 110.

2. Gene Prince, "Photography for Discovery and Scale by Superimposing Old Photographs on the Present-Day Scene," *Antiquity,* Vol. 62, no. 234 (March 1988), pp. 112–16.

3. Henry Glassie, *Folk Housing in Middle Virginia* (Knoxville: University of Tennessee Press, 1975), p. 178. Much of what is written in later chapters of this book dealing with cognition and material culture owes its form to Professor Glassie, to whom the author owes a large intellectual debt.

4. Stanley South, "Evolution and Horizon as Revealed in Ceramic Analysis in Historical Archaeology," *Conference on Historical Site Archaeology Papers* 6: 71–116 (Columbia: University of South Carolina Press, 1972).

5. Lewis Binford, "A New Method of Calculating Dates from Kaolin Pipestems," *Southeastern Archaeological Conference Newsletter,* Vol. 9, no. 1 (1961).

6. By far the best treatment of the artifactual material is Ivor

261

Noël Hume, *A Guide to the Artifacts of Colonial America* (New York: Alfred A. Knopf, 1970; New York: Vintage Books, 1991). Not only is it a thorough and detailed treatment of virtually every class of artifact likely to be encountered on a historical site in the eastern United States, but the introductory chapter should be required reading for anyone involved in historical archaeology or historical museology. With its companion volume, *Historical Archaeology* (Knopf, 1969), it should be considered as an indispensable part of the library and preparation of the historical archaeologist.

7. Cary Carson and others, "Impermanent Architecture in the Southern American Colonies," *Winterthur Portfolio* Vol. 16, nos. 2/3 (Summer/Autumn 1981), pp. 135–96.

8. For an excellent example of how folk architecture can be seen to reflect worldview, see Henry Glassie's *Folk Housing in Middle Virginia*.

9. James Deetz, *Invitation to Archaeology* (New York: Natural History Press, 1967), pp. 83–96.

2

THE ANGLO-AMERICAN PAST

1. For an account of archaeological discoveries at Flowerdew Hundred see the author's *Flowerdew Hundred: The Archaeology of a Virginia Plantation 1619–1864* (Charlottesville: University Press of Virginia, 1993).

2. William M. Kelso, *Jamestown Rediscovery I: Search for 1607 James Fort* (Jamestown, Va.: Association for the Preservation of Virginia Antiquities, 1995).

3. From 1971 through 1978 the excavations were carried out by the College of William and Mary under the direction of Professor Norman Barka, assisted by Field Director Leverett Gregory, Charles Hodges, and Andrew Edwards.

4. Ivor Noël Hume, *Martin's Hundred* (New York: Alfred A. Knopf, 1982; Charlottesville: University Press of Virginia, 1991).

in small things forgotten

5. Samuel Symonds to John Winthrop the Younger, 1638. Reprinted in Chapter 5 below.

6. For a full discussion of the evidence for bloomeries at Flowerdew Hundred see Ann B. Markell, "Manufacturing Identity: Material Culture and Social Change in Seventeenth Century Virginia" (Ph.D. diss., University of California, Berkeley, 1990).

7. Colono ware is discussed below in Chapter 8.

8. William Bradford, *Of Plimoth Plantation 1620–1647,* Samuel E. Morison, ed. (New York: Alfred A. Knopf, 1963), p. 11.

9. For a discussion of the history of this holiday, see Jay Anderson and James Deetz, "The Ethnogastronomy of Thanksgiving," *Saturday Review of Science,* November 25, 1972, pp. 29–39.

   It should be noted here that after some twenty-five years of excavating sites of seventeenth-century Plymouth, turkey bones were finally recovered from the house site of Edward Winslow (1630–50), in Marshfield, Massachusetts.

10. Alan Gowans, *Images of American Living* (Philadelphia: J. B. Lippincott, 1964), pp. 116–17.

11. Artie Rosenbaum, *Old Time Mountain Banjo* (New York: Oak Publications, 1968).

12. Henry Glassie, "Folk Art," in *Folklore and Folklife: An Introduction,* ed. Richard M. Dorson (Chicago: University of Chicago Press, 1972), pp. 268–79.

3

ALL THE EARTHENWARE PLAIN AND FLOWERED

1. Ivor Noël Hume's discussion of ceramics in *A Guide to the Artifacts of Colonial America* is the most succinct and reliable summary of American historical ceramics.

2. Jay Anderson, "A Solid Sufficiency: An Ethnography of Yeoman Foodways in Stuart England," unpublished Ph.D. dissertation, University of Pennsylvania Folklore and Folklife Department (1971), Preface, p. 2.

3. Lewis Binford, "Archaeology as Anthropology," *American Antiquity,* Vol. 28, no. 2 (October 1962), pp. 217–26.

4. Jay Anderson, "A Solid Sufficiency: An Ethnography of Yeoman Foodways in Stuart England."

5. Marley Brown III, "Ceramics from Plymouth, 1621–1800: The Documentary Record," in Ian Quimby, ed., *Ceramics in America,* Winterthur Conference Report (Wilmington, Del.: Winterthur Museum, 1972), pp. 41–74.

6. Ivor Noël Hume, *A Guide to the Artifacts of Colonial America,* p. 108.

7. *Virginia Magazine of History and Biography,* Vol. 15 (1908), p. 31.

4

REMEMBER ME AS YOU PASS BY

1. Harriette M. Forbes, *Gravestones of Early New England and the Men Who Made Them, 1653–1800* (Boston: Houghton Mifflin, 1927; New York: Da Capo Press, 1967).

2. James A. Ford, *A Quantitative Method for Deriving Cultural Chronology* (Washington, D.C.: Pan-American Union, 1962).

3. The earlier date, 1680, represents the time from which sufficient numbers of stones have survived to provide a sample of adequate size to study quantitatively. After 1820, gravestone carving had become the full-time occupation of most stone carvers in the region. As a result, a new set of factors was at work on design selection and transmission, and gravestone carving had entered the realm of popular culture.

4. Alan Ludwig, *Graven Images* (Middletown, Conn.: Wesleyan University Press, 1966).

5. James Deetz and Edwin Dethlefsen, "The Doppler Effect and Archaeology: A Consideration of the Spatial Aspects of Seriation," *Southwestern Journal of Anthropology,* Vol. 21, no. 3 (1965), pp. 196–206.

6. Peter Benes, *The Masks of Orthodoxy: Folk Gravestone Carving*

in Plymouth County, Massachusetts, 1689–1805 (Amherst: University of Massachusetts Press, 1977), p. 70.

7. Peter Benes, "Nathaniel Fuller, Stonecutter of Plympton, Massachusetts," *Old Time New England,* Society for the Preservation of New England Antiquities, Boston, Vol. 60, no. 1 (1969), pp. 12–30.

8. Ibid.

5

I WOULD HAVE THE HOWSE STRONGE

1. William Bradford, *History of Plymouth Plantation, 1620–1647,* 2 vols. (Boston: Massachusetts Historical Society, 1912), Vol. 2, pp. 214–15.

2. Robert Blair St. George, " 'Set Thine House in Order': The Domestication of the Yeomanry in Seventeenth-Century New England," in *Common Places: Readings in American Vernacular Architecture,* eds. Dell Upton and John Michael Vlach (Athens: University of Georgia Press, 1986), p. 347.

3. Roland Robbins and Evan Jones, *Pilgrim John Alden's Progress: Archaeological Excavations in Duxbury* (Plymouth, Mass.: The Pilgrim Society, 1969).

4. Samuel Symonds, letter to John Winthrop the Younger, 1638. *Collections of the Massachusetts Historical Society,* 4th ser., Vol. 7 (1865), pp. 118–20.

5. Hugh Morrison, *Early American Architecture* (New York: Oxford University Press, 1952), pp. 279–80.

6. James Deetz and others, "Plymouth Colony Room-by-Room Inventories, 1633–1684." Unpublished paper. Abstracted in *Early American Probate Inventories* (Boston: Dublin Seminar for New England Folklife Annual Proceedings, Vol. 12, 1987), p. 182.

7. Cecil A. Hewett, "Some East Anglian Prototypes for Early Timber Houses in America," *Post Medieval Archaeology,* Vol. 3 (1970), pp. 100–21.

8. Harold Shurtleff, *The Log Cabin Myth* (Cambridge, Mass.: Harvard University Press, 1939).

9. Fraser D. Neiman, *The "Manner House" Before Stratford: Discovering the Clifts Plantation* (Stratford, Va.: Robert E. Lee Memorial Association, 1980), pp. 31–32.

10. Robert Blair St. George, "Maintenance Relations and the Erotics of Property in Historical Thought." Unpublished mss.

11. Dell Upton, "The Origin of Chesapeake Architecture," in *Three Centuries of Maryland Architecture* (Annapolis: Maryland Historical Trust, 1982), pp. 44–57.

12. Ibid., p. 48.

13. Fraser D. Neiman, "Domestic Architecture at the Clifts Plantation: The Social Context of Early Virginia Building," in *Common Places: Readings in American Vernacular Architecture,* eds. Dell Upton and John Michael Vlach, p. 314, note 51.

14. Lila O'Neale, *Yurok-Karok Basket Weavers,* Publications in American Archaeology and Ethnology, Vol. 32, no. 1 (Berkeley: University of California Press, 1932).

6

SMALL THINGS REMEMBERED

1. Geoffrey Moran, "Trash Pits and Natural Rights in the Revolutionary Era," *Archaeology,* Vol. 29, no. 3 (July 1976), pp. 144–202.

2. Anne Yentsch, "Understanding Seventeenth and Eighteenth Century Colonial Families: An Experiment in Historical Ethnography." Unpublished M.A. thesis, Brown University, Department of Anthropology, 1975.

3. Eric Davidson and Paul Newman, "Bluegrass from the Blue Ridge," Folkways Records, monograph accompanying record Fs 3832, *Band Music from Grayson and Carroll Counties, Va. A Half Century of Change,* New York, 1967.

4. Ibid., p. 5.

5. Ibid., p. 9.

6. Bernard Bailyn, *The New England Merchants in the Seventeenth Century* (Cambridge, Mass.: Harvard University Press, 1955), pp. 91–114.

7
PARTING WAYS

1. John Vlach, "Shotgun Houses," *Natural History,* Vol. 87, no. 2 (1977), pp. 50–57.

2. Sibyl Moholy-Nagy, *Native Genius in Autonomous Architecture* (New York: Horizon Press, 1957), p. 120.

3. The following discussion is based on work done under the direction of Marley Brown III and presented by Constance Crosby and Matthew C. Emerson in a paper, "Identifying Afro-American Mortuary Customs: An Example from Parting Ways Settlement, Plymouth, Massachusetts," at the Annual Meeting of the Society for Historical Archaeology held in Nashville, Tennessee, in January 1979.

4. William Faulkner, *Go Down Moses* (New York: Random House, 1955), p. 135. Quoted by John Vlach in *The Afro-American Tradition in Decorative Arts* (Athens: University of Georgia Press, 1990), p. 139.

5. John Vlach, *The Afro-American Tradition in Decorative Arts,* p. 141.

8
THE AFRICAN AMERICAN PAST

1. Mechal Sobel, *The World They Made Together: Black and White Values in Eighteenth-Century Virginia* (Princeton, N.J.: Princeton University Press, 1987), p. 5.

2. Ibid., p. 8.

3. John Vlach, *The Afro-American Tradition in Decorative Arts,* pp. 123–31.

4. John Vlach, "Shotgun Houses," p. 57.

5. John Vlach, *The Afro-American Tradition in Decorative Arts,* p. 125.

6. Leland Ferguson, *Uncommon Ground: Archaeology and Early African America 1650–1800* (Washington, D.C.: Smithsonian Institution Press, 1992).

7. William M. Kelso, *Kingsmill Plantations, 1619–1800: Archaeology of Country Life in Colonial Virginia* (San Diego: Academic Press, 1984).

8. John Vlach, *The Afro-American Tradition in Decorative Arts,* p. 125.

9. William Thorndale, "The Virginia Census of 1619," *Magazine of Virginia Genealogy,* Vol. 33, No. 3 (1995), pp. 155–70. Prior to the publication of this article, it was thought that the first Africans to arrive in English America were the twenty-odd brought by a Dutch privateer in August 1619, and the historiography of the period universally reflects this. But, based on this evidence, Thorndale says that the presence of thirty-two Africans in Virginia before August of 1619 suggests that "the Colony first acquired African labor earlier and more deliberately than implied by the chance appearance of a Dutch privateer" (p. 166).

10. Mechal Sobel, *The World They Made Together,* p. 119.

11. Dell Upton, "Vernacular Architecture (Lowland South)," in *The Encyclopedia of Southern Culture,* eds. Charles Reagan Wilson and William Ferris (New York: Anchor Books, 1991), Vol. 1, p. 187.

12. Dell Upton, "Traditional Timber Framing: An Interpretive Essay," in *The Material Culture of the Wooden Age,* ed. Ed. Brooke Hindle (New York: Tarrytown, 1981), p. 51.

13. Henry Glassie, *Folk Housing in Middle Virginia,* p. 137.

14. John Vlach, *The Afro-American Tradition in Decorative Arts,* p. 136.

15. Vlach quoting Pierce Lewis, ibid., p. 137.

16. Quoted by Fiske Kimball in his *Domestic Architecture of the*

American Colonies and of the Early Republic (New York: Dover, 1966 reprint of 1922 edition), pp. 98–99.

17. John Solomon Otto, *Cannon's Point Plantation, 1794–1860: Living Conditions and Status Patterns in the Old South* (New York: Academic Press, 1984).

18. George L. Miller, "Classification and Economic Scaling of 19th Century Ceramics," *Historical Archaeology,* Vol. 14 (1980), p. 4.

19. Ivor Noël Hume, "An Indian Ware of the Colonial Period," Archaeological Society of Virginia *Quarterly Bulletin,* Vol. 17, no. 1 (1962), pp. 1–12.

20. Richard R. Polhemus, *Archaeological Investigations of the Tellico Blockhouse Site (40MR50): A Federal Military and Trade Complex* (Report submitted to the Tennessee Valley Authority, 1977), published as TVA Reports in Anthropology, no. 16, p. 258.

21. Leland Ferguson, "Looking for the 'Afro' in Colono-Indian Pottery," in *Archaeological Perspectives on Ethnicity in America,* ed. Robert L. Schuyler (Farmingdale, N.Y.: Baywood, 1980), pp. 14–28.

22. For a more detailed and extended discussion of Colono ware see the author's *Flowerdew Hundred,* pp. 79–91.

23. Thomas Jefferson, *Notes on the State of Virginia,* ed. William Peden (Chapel Hill: University of North Carolina Press, 1955), pp. 96–97.

24. Ivor Noël Hume, "An Indian Ware of the Colonial Period."

25. Susan L. Henry, "Terra-Cotta Tobacco Pipes in 17th Century Maryland and Virginia: A Preliminary Study," *Historical Archaeology,* Vol. 13 (1979), pp. 14–37.

26. Edmund S. Morgan, *American Slavery American Freedom: The Ordeal of Colonial Virginia* (New York: Norton, 1975), p. 155.

index

in South Carolina, 218–19,
225–26
Turner-Burr house, 194–98,
195, 202, 203, 222–23
two-room houses, 222–23
in Virginia, 219–21, 223–25
African Americans, 5–6, 187–
88
creolization and, 213–14
European attitudes toward,
250–51
grave decoration practices,
207–10
gravestone art, 112–13, *113*
material culture of, 212–13
See also Parting Ways site;
Slavery
African cultural survival, 200–
1, 252
in foodways, 243
in housing, 215–19, 222–23,
226
at Parting Ways site, 199–
210
in pipe-making, 246–48
African influences on Anglo-
American domestic
architecture, 226–31
Agrarian lifeway, persistence
of, 175
Akan people, 209
Alden, John, 39
Alden house, 202
Allerton, Isaac, 133
Allyn house, 144
Anderson, Jay, 73, 76
Anglo-American culture, 6
ceramics and, 76, 85–86

domestic architecture and,
140–41
first period (pre-1680), 58–60
gravestone art and, 121–24
peasants and, 61–62
second period (1680–1760),
60–62
third period (post–1760),
62–64, 66–67
Annular ware, 234–35
Archaeology, 4
dimensions of archaeological
data, 89–90
horizon concept, 64
postmedieval archaeology, 6
salvage archaeology, 44–49
tradition concept, 64, 65
See also Historical
archaeology; Prehistoric
archaeology
Architecture
regional variation in
architectural forms, 48
See also Domestic
architecture
Artifacts. *See* Material culture
Asian Americans, 6
Attire, regulation of, 81–82
Australopithecine man-apes,
125

Bacon's Castle, 149
Bagpipes, 176
Bailey, Colonel John, 189
Ballads, 177
Banjos, 2–3, 65, 178–79, 180
Barbados, 225, 239
Barker, William, 50, 56–57

index

about the author

James Deetz is a professor of historical archaeology at the University of Virginia. He has taught at the University of California at Santa Barbara, Harvard, Brown, William and Mary, the University of Cape Town, and the University of California, Berkeley, where he won the Distinguished Teaching Award. Mr. Deetz received his B.A., M.A., and Ph.D. degrees from Harvard and is the author of several previous books, including *Invitation to Archaeology* and *Flowerdew Hundred*. He lives in Charlottesville, Virginia.